SOPHIA WILLIAMS

I'M GOOD

My Struggle

My Fight

My Breakthrough

SOPHIA WILLIAMS

I'M GOOD

My Struggle

My Fight

My Breakthrough

TATE PUBLISHING
AND ENTERPRISES, LLC

Published by Tate Publishing & Enterprises, LLC
127 E. Trade Center Terrace | Mustang, Oklahoma 73064 USA
1.888.361.9473 | www.tatepublishing.com

Tate Publishing is committed to excellence in the publishing industry. The company reflects the philosophy established by the founders, based on Psalm 68:11,
"The Lord gave the word and great was the company of those who published it."

Book design copyright © 2013 by Tate Publishing, LLC. All rights reserved.
Cover design by Rtor Maghuyop
Interior design by Joana Quilantang

Published in the United States of America

ISBN: 978-1-62510-797-8
1. Biography & Autobiography / Personal Memoirs
2. Biography & Autobiography / General
13.01.11

ACKNOWLEDGMENT

I want to say first and foremost, thanks be to God for allowing me this opportunity to share my story with others. If it wasn't for him and the strength that he has given me, I would have remained silent like so many others that have been through and are going through the things I mentioned in this book. I have three guardian angels in my life I would like to thank personally. Deborah Ford, Wesley Ford and Mary Anderson, thank you all for always being there for me through everything. If it was not for your help love and support I don't know where I would be. For your graciousness and generosity I thank all of you from the bottom of my heart. I love all of you and hope that I make it above and beyond my wildest imaginations so that I can give back to you guys, as much as you given to me. Without my three guardian angels, I probably would have given up a long time ago. Thank you.

INTRO

There are a lot of philosophical sayings that society has made up. They are most often used when someone is complaining or experiencing a "life" situation. One saying that I'm going to have to disagree with is that "life is what you make it." Life is actually whatever comes your way. You just have to deal with whatever comes. We don't choose rather or not we want to be born; we don't choose who our parents are. We don't choose our first school or how others treat us. So no, life is *not* what you make it.

My feelings are so strong about this saying because my life was completely planned. I must say the coordinator who planned my life did a horrible job planning it out. I really haven't had the best twenty-four years. When I try to make it better, it seems to get worse. When I think I'm happy, life shows me it's only temporary. When I try to force it, I fail to succeed.

The point of this story is to encourage and let others know that everyone has some type of story. Some stories might be sad, unpleasant, or plain depressing. Remember, someone else has probably experienced the same, if not worse. My saying is "Never let your past determine your future." Me personally, I try to live up to *my beliefs*.

CHAPTER 1

July 1, 1987 was the day I was born to a woman who wasn't quite ready to have children. My mother had a boy about thirteen months before my birth. I was her second child. With me being an added responsibility, the odds were already against me. I was born in Milwaukee, Wisconsin, at the Macomb County Health Department. My mom had originally been living in Detroit, Michigan, about a year before she gave birth to me. A few months after my birth, my mom decided to head back home to Detroit. Unfortunately, my mother got pregnant again about a year and a half after having me. Having three kids all under the age of four in diapers, screaming and yelling, has to be a handful. A lot of residents fall prey to the predators that contribute to the downfall of the city. My mom was one of their victims.

I can't remember too much from when I was one or two. No one can remember too much from such a long time ago unless they were blessed with a unique gift of remembrance. There are a few things that I do remember about that part of my life. The things I do remember are faint, and some things might even be a figment of my imagination. One of the main things I do remember for a fact is my mom leaving me, my brother, and sister alone in the apartment for plenty of nights.

My mother would leave the TV on whenever she decided she wanted to leave. That was her way of keeping us "distracted" and hopefully out of trouble. My mother would feed and bathe us and head out to do whatever she felt. My brother and I would just sit side by side and watch whatever show my mom put on the television. I was in love with Miss Piggy of the Muppets, so that was my show of preference. We would watch TV and fall asleep or lie awake waiting for my mom to return.

Another faint memory I have, which is more or less a figment of my imagination, was me seeing a mouse the size of a human come through our apartment wall. This mouse was gigantic, hairy, and terrifying. I think what had really happened was that I'd been taken to the kids' play place Chuck E. Cheese. I think I happened to see a mouse running around sometime later on in the apartment. I believe that in my small mind, I took the live Chuck E. mouse and put him in place of the small rodent.

Eventually, after so many nights of being left alone, it became noticeable. The neighbors began to peep and question how my mom was always leaving when no one was ever coming into her home. They knew she had children and noticed we weren't leaving out the house with her. The neighbors became concerned and suspicious. Someone who actually cared finally decided to call the police.

Two women, I assume neighbors, came to my mother's apartment (she left the door unlocked) and took us out of the home. CPS and the police became involved in the situation. The night we were taken from our home, it was pretty late, so the police came and got us because there were no state workers available that late. We were put in the back of cruiser and taken to the station where we were to stay overnight until a worker could be reached. The next day, we were put into a foster home. We became temporary wards of the state.

So at two years old, I no longer had a mother. Some lose their mother to cancer, murder, or prison; I lost my mother to drugs. Drugs are what made her leave us at home alone. Drugs are what had her not thinking about the outcome of her choices. What if we had went into a cabinet and drunk some cleaning fluids, what if the house was on fire, or what if someone had broken in, there would have been no one around to rescue us. We could have ended up dead.

The foster home wasn't the best. Being able to have visits with my mother at the foster care agency was the greatest. Even though the visits were only once a week, that one time was all I needed. I was happy and content with just that one time. It was the one time I would smile and feel happiness. My mom would always bring snacks and goodies with her every time she came to see us. I was too young to know what was going on, so I never cried or acted out during or after the visit.

The foster mom me and my brother were placed with did not have any kids in the home. I don't know if she had any older biological children or not. From the way she treated us emotionally and physically, I don't believe she had any kids of her own. She was a mean woman that always yelled and stayed upset about everything me and my brother did. One issue that occurred that got the state involved was a time when she whooped my three-year-old brother with a vacuum hose. We were immediately taken and replaced.

The visits continued with my mom, my brother, and my younger sister. My sister was taken and put into another foster home, separated from me and my brother. I wasn't too happy about that. I loved having a baby sister. They allowed all of us to have our visits together so that we could see my sister. While feeling the moments of happiness with my mother at the visits, I was feeling fear and hesitancy when leaving to go back to my new foster home. I dreaded leaving the agency after my visit with my mom.

CHAPTER 2

My new foster mom was a devil in the flesh. I would have to say the state did not make a good decision with their next choice of placement. I think they were annoyed and just wanted to be done with our case. Time is money, and the one thing they did not want to spend was money. The state did not take the time or effort to ensure we were put somewhere decent. The only good thing was that I and my brother were once again placed together. My sister, however, was kept with the same family.

Ms. Jonsas was a younger foster mom. She looked as if she was in her mid thirties with hairy legs. She had a very nice home; it was set on the corner of the block. If you've ever been to Detroit, you would know that majority of the homes are brick houses with some vinyl or aluminum siding. Her home was a medium-sized light brown brick home. It had a medium front yard and a large backyard with a play set. By this time, I was just barely three years old, so I couldn't wait to get on that play set. The first time I got on it, I fell and scraped the whole bottom side of my face. I still have a faint scar to this day.

Any how, Ms. Jonsas had a bunch of kids in her adequately sized home. It seemed as if she had more kids than she did space. There were about four boys in the home and one girl. One of the rooms at the end of the hallway had one wooden bunk bed; the room across from it had two sets. The room with one bunk was the girls' room and the other room was for the boys. I was taken into my room where my foster mom unpacked my things and put them in the drawers and closet. I was made to sleep on the bottom bunk because I was the youngest girl, and I was likely to fall out the top bunk. The inside of the home was well decorated and tidy. She had the type of house where you would be scared to touch anything because everything was so spotless and fancy.

Now, of course, everything started off okay. The honeymoon period was for a good month or less. As time went by, true colors began to shine through. The mask was taken off, and I was able to see the real her. It was not a pretty sight. Ms. Jonsas was abusive with a sharp and hurtful tongue. She would say and do things just to hurt my feelings. It was as if she liked to see me cry. Her day consisted of working and coming home to mess with me. She was like a playground bully.

Our visits continued with our mom every week. That was the only escape we had to get out of her evil foster grip. Going back home was hard every time, knowing what was in store for us. Ms. Jonsas did anything she could to torture me and my brother. Sometimes Ms. Jonsas could be nice. She would let me go places with her and watch music videos in her room. My favorite song at that time was H-Town's "Knockin' the Boots," which should've been ABCs or some nursery rhymes, but she never played that type of music. I would sing and dance around in her room to every old school song that came on her TV.

She would be that way one moment and cruel the next—like lights on, lights off, change, just like that. One instance of her cruelty was the day I was eating a spaghetti dinner. I accidentally dropped some of my noodles and meat on the floor. I tried to pick up as much meat and noodles off the floor as I could, but the noodles were slippery. The spaghetti was very saucy, so as a three-year-old child using a fork, I had a hard time keeping it on the utensil. Ms. Jonsas saw that I dropped the spaghetti on her clean black-and-white tile and was pissed. She looked at me with such aggravation and annoyance. She told me that I needed to lick the spot up I'd made my mess on. So instead of being handed a paper towel or a cloth rag, I was forced to lick the floor.

Not only did Ms. Jonsas pick, so did the other kids. My brother and I were constantly pushed, teased, and harassed. The older boys that lived in the home made it a habit to touch and hump on me all the time. I remember experiencing my first butterflies when I was around three or four years old. Years later, I discovered those same boys were also sexually abusing my brother. The teasing went from the home and continued on to the school. My brother and I would be severely picked on and messed with on our way home from school. We attended the same school that our foster care siblings were in. Our foster siblings knew the kids at the school already, so they made up rumors and talked about us to other kids, thus, causing us to be teased outside the home as well.

I remember being sick and scared almost every day of my life there. I hated going to school. I hated going home. I hated knowing I was going to see my mom but not leave with her. It was a very tough time for me. I struggled with stomachaches and dizziness. Instead of Ms. Jonsas trying to discover what was wrong (by taking me to the doctor), she would just give me Vernors. It never worked, so I was always sick and laying around tired and nauseated.

I went to bed sad every night and woke up sad every morning. Every night I had nightmares. I would always see my predators in my dreams, and my mind painted pictures of them on my window. I was living a nightmare every day during the day, and at night in my dreams. I was too young to be so unhappy, and no one cared.

I seem to remember getting shots quite often. It seemed like every week I was getting a needle poked into me. The other siblings at the foster home would tease me about my discomfort and pain. Ms. Jonsas would laugh right along with them while telling them to stop teasing me. I would just look and roll my eyes at all of them because I found nothing to be funny. Now that I'm older, I'm guessing I was probably receiving some vaccinations. I was probably not up-to-date on most of my required vaccines.

My visits with my mom continued on; the months went by slowly. Eventually it turned into a year, then years, and I was still in the same home. Every time I would visit my mom she'd have a different dye color in her hair; it was one or a bunch of different colors— she would have colorful hair in each visit. I loved to see the new colors she would put in her. The colors made her face and skin stand out, and her changing hair colors were associated with my most vivid memories of her face.

Around the holidays, my mom would always bring me and my siblings' gifts and candies to match the theme of that holiday. The foster care agency always hosted holiday potlucks, and the parents would bring in a dish or some type of edible contribution to the holiday dinner. My mom's favorite dish that she always brought was her infamous spaghetti. She could make the best spaghetti. Her spaghetti was a saucy dish— thick, full of meat, and swimming in shredded cheese. I loved that woman's spaghetti!

While I enjoyed my holidays with my mom and my siblings and other agency families, I was still living with Ms. Jonsas—being molested, abused, and teased. There was no one I could tell because our worker was not very involved in our lives there. When we went to the agency, we were immediately put in a room with our mother. There was no chance to talk to anyone. Being the age I was, I didn't know what to say if I did have the opportunity to tell someone. I didn't know that what I was going through was wrong and inappropriate.

I lost my first tooth sometime around the age of five. I did not lose my tooth the average way a child's tooth falls out. My gums were still pretty hard and encased around the tooth; it had not begun to hang loosely from my gums just yet. That particular day, I was being watched by my foster mom's older niece, Pumpkin. Pumpkin was fat and mean just like the others. She abused her authority; any opportunity she had, rather necessary or not, she would hit me and my brother. Pumpkin saw that my tooth had just begun to loosen up at the top. She took her fat fist and punched me in my mouth to knock it all the way out. My mouth was bleeding; my gums and lips were aching. She just sent me to bed, snaggletoothed, hurting, and crying.

Pumpkin was an ugly big girl that did not have much hair. I was a pretty little girl with long, fine, straight hair. Now that I'm older and can look back on how she treated me, I believe that she had been jealous of me. At five years old, my hair hung past my shoulders while she was a grown woman with short, nappy hair. One day, while Ms. Jonsas was out doing whatever, Pumpkin took it into her own hands to try and perm my hair. Now, most know what perms are used for. For those that don't, it's used to straighten out kinky, thick, unmanageable hair. Pumpkin put the perm in, and I lost a good portion of my hair; the remaining hair was left damaged, broken, and rough.

That was the first time my foster mom took up for me or cared about anything that happened to me.

My foster mom was upset that the babysitter touched my hair without her permission, and she noticed my tooth was missing already. Ms. Jonsas was pissed that Pumpkin ruined my hair; she asked her repeatedly where she got the nerve to touch my head in the first place. Pumpkin tried to make it seem as if she was trying to do me a favor. Ms. Jonsas saw right through her lie. Pumpkin was yelled and screamed at while being cursed out and scorned for her actions. When I told Ms. Jonsas the entire story of what took place that day, Pumpkin was never allowed to watch me or my brother again. I believe that the only reason why Ms. Jonsas was upset about my hair being gone was because she enjoyed playing it and putting it up in ponytails all over my head.

I was with Ms. Jonsas for two and a half to three years. I went through years of abuse, neglect, and shame. During these three years of my struggle, my mom was still struggling with meeting her requirements to get custody back. She still had not gotten herself together. We'd been visiting her for a while and had plenty of time. I guess some people have a harder time doing the right thing than others. She had not fulfilled the requirements or taken the necessary steps she needed to gain full custody back. By the end of those three years, they'd given her to pull it all together; my mom was once again pregnant with her fourth child.

My mom now had me, my brother, my sister, and a fetus growing inside her. I remember playing and rubbing on her belly. I remember her trying to lift me up to the water fountain at the agency and I could feel her big ole belly behind me. I loved asking her for a hug or laying on her so I could feel the baby move around in her stomach. It made me feel loved and close to her. Some people have asked why she had more children knowing she couldn't or didn't want to take care of them. I'd love to know myself. Only she can answer that question.

A memory of my mom before they ended the visits was a happy but somewhat sad one. My mom always seemed sad or down. I think it was because she was hurting, knowing she couldn't pull herself together and was about to lose us forever. She tried to keep her spirits up for our sake, but young children can feel when something is not right with someone they love. It's like a sixth sense children have that adults don't know about. They can see things and feel things that an adult cannot recognize. I had that sixth sense; I knew something wasn't right with my mom or with our situation.

I think even though I was young, my mind was mature for my age. I began to realize near the end that this was it, I was going to lose my mom forever. I began to become very sad and anxious because I knew what was to come. The last few visits before the separation from my mom and sister were the worst. Our family caseworker told me and my brother that we were no longer going to see our mother.

I began to act out during the last few visits—crying, picking on my older brother and my younger sister (the baby was not born yet), and yelling at my mom. I was six by this time, so I had quite the vocabulary. I remember quite vividly yelling at my mother and telling her I did not love her. She just looked at me with tears in her eyes. I never saw my mom or my little sister again. My mom was still pregnant up until the split-up, so I never saw my unborn sister either.

The visits ended, and so did my happiness and my life. My brother and I began to visit with a family from out of town—the Robinsons. The Robinsons were an older strict couple who were thinking about adopting us. The visits started out with them sitting with us in the agency, talking and trying to build a bond. They would bring gifts and sweets to lure us into liking them. They were doing a good job, I was stubborn and bitter because of everything that had happened, but I began to open up to the both of them.

After so many mandatory agency meetings, the Robinsons were allowed to take us out and about. They mainly took us to McDonald's, where we would get a happy meal and play in the play place. They seemed like very nice people, very talkative and friendly. They looked mean because of the wrinkles and line in their faces, so I was a little nervous. I figured old people are sweet people even if they do look a little stern, and they give you kisses and candies all the time.

There were a couple of months of in-town visits; the Robinsons were granted permission to take us to their city for overnight visits. The Robinsons were from a smaller city not too far from Detroit, Michigan. They were from Grand Rapids, which was about three hours away from where we lived. I realized that during one of those last overnight visits, that life was not about to get any better. Sometimes, as I stated, a child can just sense something's not right. That last visit stirred up my senses, and I knew something was wrong or was going to be wrong.

This was the last weekend visit before the adoption was finalized. Now due to the history of my life, I had a few issues. Who wouldn't have some type of problems or issues after going through what I had went through? One of the issues I had was incompetency due to nervousness resulting from a change of atmosphere. My last overnight visit at the Robinson apartment was a scary one. Just knowing that I was going to be "there" for the rest of my life was a big event. That last night visit, I peed my bed.

By the time I woke up, I was completely dry. After getting up and notifying the Robinsons we were awoke, I was told to go back to my room and wait for them to get up. I went back into the room and me and my brother just sat there talking about what our new life might be like. Mrs. Robinson got up and entered our room some time later with her husband and greeted me and my brother. She gave each of us a hug and said good morning then began to make the beds.

There were bunk beds in the room that me and my brother had slept in that night. My brother had slept at the bottom, me, on the top. I don't know why I had been told to sleep at the top with me being the youngest. I figured maybe because the bottom bunk was full-sized and my brother was older, so he should get the bigger bed. Mrs. Robinson started to fix the sheets on the bottom then began to straighten out the covers on the top bunk. She paused, looked at me, and asked if I had peed the bed.

I stated that I had not wet the bed. She asked me a few more times, "Are you sure?" I replied, "Yes, I am." She told me to come and look at the covers I slept on. There was a big yellow stain with a brown outline around it. She began to lecture me immediately, saying that she and her husband were Christian people, and they did not allow lying in their home. If looks could kill, you would not be reading this story today.

Several weeks later, the adoption was signed, sealed, and finalized. The Robinsons were ordained to be my new parents. It was now a long-term, lifelong contract—something that a young child had no control over. I just had to go wherever they decided to stick me at. It was a lifelong contract that I wish I got the pleasure of deciding on.

Ms. Jonsas gathered me and my brother's things and put them in garbage bags, so we were ready to go when the Robinsons arrived. The Robinsons came to Ms. Jonsas's house and packed our things into their black-and-pink van had us say our good-byes to everyone and jumped on the highway for the three-hour ride home. After that last visit, I knew I was in for a long haul, and I was scared.

CHAPTER 3

The Robinsons lived in a two-bedroom apartment. It was a subsidized living community with kids everywhere. The apartment complex was decent and big with lots of open fields for playing. Mrs. Robinson's adult daughter stayed three apartments down from us. She had about four boys, all of whom was around me and my brother's age category. Mrs. Robinson also had a young lady that she mentored through her church who stayed on the other side of the complex. That lady had about three kids around our age as well. One girl and two boys, I believe. She was a very nice lady. However, Mrs. Robinson's daughter was not very accepting of us.

The Robinsons played it cool in the beginning, but there were moments that just weren't right. Mrs. Robinson immediately ordered us to call her mom and Mr. Robinson dad. We hadn't even been there for a complete month yet. She didn't give us a chance to get to know her better and adapt to her.

There was no establishment of our comfort ability with our recent adoption or with having to call them mom and dad. Whenever we did slip up and call her Mrs. Robinsons, she would say so calmly, but with the sternest voice, that her name was mom, not Mrs. Robinson. She stated that she would not continue to repeat herself; we would be disciplined if we kept slipping up.

We were adopted during one of the summer months, so our first couple of months were spent mostly outside. We played with Mrs. Robinson's daughter, sons, and the other lady's kids. We were always rolling down the big hill by our side of the complex, bike riding, and engaging in hide-and-seek games.

Sundays were considered to be an in-home day. Besides going to church and eating out occasionally, Sundays were days of rest and pure laziness. Watching TV and movies and lying around is what majority of our Sundays consisted of.

Not too soon after taking my brother and me in, the Robinsons decided to take in a young woman named Fancy from their church to live with us. She became a makeshift nanny. Mrs. Robinson was an elder in the church, and it was her duty to look out for the church members. She decided to adopt her into the church as family and outside the church into her home as a daughter.

Fancy's duties were to watch us when the Robinsons were running errands, to feed us, and to keep us in line. She was really taken in to be used for taking care of us. She was nice at the beginning as well. Looks and first impressions can be very deceiving; that's why they say don't judge a book by its cover.

After about a year of living in the subsidized housing community, we moved from our two-bedroom apartment to a five-bedroom house in an urban community. We upgraded from a nineties van to an Eddie Bauer Expedition matching the current year. The Robinsons were buying all types of things left and right, they were living well. Funny thing is, nothing was bought for me and my brother. We received our things from Goodwill and thrift stores—if we received anything.

Mrs. Robinson became greedy with her newfound wealth and became extremely physically abusive. No matter how small any situation or behavior, we were always punished rather by touch or nonphysical discipline. My childhood had already been whisked away, now my life was beginning to be snatched from me as well. Every other day, I was either in a corner or being hit. She was taking her authority over us above and beyond where it needed to be. She was power happy and abusing her position of power.

Originally, punishments would mean standing in the corner for the day—sometimes with my hands on my head, sometimes with one leg up, depending on how she felt. That must not have been enough for Mrs. Robinson. She than began to pull hair, whip me, and torture me and my brother. She became a crazy and abusive, money-hungry maniac. It was as if she needed to hear or see us in utter pain and discomfort. If she was a real monster, not just theoretically speaking, she would've had the strength of a bull. She fed off of our misery.

Mrs. Robinson (Mr. Robinson was not involved in her antics, a man of few words) knew I was terrified of the dark, and she'd always use that against me. On plenty of occasions, instead of having me stand in front of my bedroom door or whipping me, she would place me into a dark corner in the attic.

Almost every day after school, I was placed in that scary dark corner. I would just close my eyes and cry, open them, and look all around, hoping I wouldn't see a spider, a monster, or a ghost. I can't remember any of the things I did to get put in that attic dang near every day.

Going to school should have been a time where I was excited to get away. Not only was being at home hell on earth, being at school was hell as well. Mrs. Robinson did not allow us to wear different clothes to school. We were made to wear the same outfit for a full week.

If you stained it, you might get lucky and be able to wear something different the next day. We went to school looking like poor kids, but we were far from it. Our appearance caused a lot of judgmental stares and assumptions. We were considered uncool and outcasts.

I always wore frilly, flowery looking clothes with older hairstyles. I would have a little bun with a double flip bang or something like that. On a daily basis, children teased and treated me and my brother like we were disgusting creatures. They talked about our dirty clothes and thought we were weird.

We weren't weird, we were scared. We had endured and were still living a horrible life. The children at the school were bad kids. They cursed and picked fights with each other all the time. Drugs were sold on the playgrounds. It was a horrible school in a low-class community.

I got into my first forced fight in the third grade. There was this girl I never hung out with or knew that wanted to fight me. I tried to avoid the situation, knowing that if I engaged in it, the fight back home would be worse. There was an older playground attendant there who saw the commotion and came over. She asked what was going on. When she was told, she took it upon herself to snatch my coat and backpack and push me into the middle of the crowd. She told me I better fight the girl, to not be scared of her.

I couldn't believe I was being forced by a grown up to fight. So I fought the girl because I was right in front of her in the crowd. I couldn't let her just hit on me without retaliating. She had some weave braids in her hair, and I guess I pulled a few out because some were found the next day on the school yard. She wanted to fight me again, but she was talked out of it.

Going home after school, almost constantly, I was picked on again by Mrs. Robinson who would find something to fuss at me about as soon as I got through the door. It was always something—if not this than that. She was never satisfied or content with anything I did or said. She was a woman, who believed everything should be done exactly the way she wanted, but we were kids, nothing could be done exactly to her expectations.

If I left a wrinkle in my bed, I was placed on corner punishment for about two or three days. If I had a stain on my clothes when I got home, I was made to immediately go to a corner as if I stained it on purpose. Any small mistake that could be made had a punishment to go with it, no matter what.

The plastic spatula used to hit the back of my hand was her favorite. I can't count how many times I was told to hold my hand out, knuckles up, and be hit with that spatula. Somehow she had discovered that the backs of the hand being smacked hurt worse than the inside.

I never said anything to anybody. I had no idea that I was being mistreated. I had lived through abuse for years before I made it to her home. I thought every kid lived the way I lived. I'd never been shown anything else to believe otherwise. It was natural to me.

Mrs. Robinson's other forms of punishment were just pure unethical and unnecessary. Even food was being used as a part of her torture spree. Depending on how she felt that day, you could either get a whooping or be made to eat cold, clammy, plain oatmeal.

The recipe for the oatmeal was plain oatmeal in the round tall container cooked in boiling water, taken out, put into a bowl, and placed into the freezer or refrigerator. She would let it sit in the refrigerator for a few hours then take it out and let it sit until it became gucky and clammy. If you threw up in it, you were to eat it. I made that mistake one time.

If you weren't in the corner for a punishment, you were eating plain peanut butter sandwiches for a week with dry carrots and no water for dinner. Or she would decide to add beets to the oatmeal specialty. Plenty of times you would just be sent to bed with a burning, growling stomach with no food or water in it. She did not care about our nutritional health in any way. Anything and everything she could think of that was below evil, she thought of it and acted on it.

Approximately about a year or two later, the Robinsons adopted a pair of siblings. They had decided to get a girl and two boys. The children were a tad bit younger than me and my brother, but not too far behind. One of the boys was four, the other was one, and the little girl was two years old. The youngest boy was extremely small for his age; he did not look healthy at all.

You could tell he was malnourished; he was so skinny it looked as if he was withering away. That did not stop Ms. Robinson from putting her hands on the small boy. Their abuse was started not too long after being taken in mainly because Mrs. Robinson was comfortable that she had not been caught in the amount of time she'd had us, so why change?

The little girl, Yasmine, was absolutely beautiful. She had long, beautiful curly hair and a golden skin complexion. She was believed to be from a different ethnicity because of her exotic appearance. She was treated the best out of all the kids in the home. I hate to say, but I believe Mrs. Robinson did not touch her because she was pretty.

I believe her unique beauty saved her quite a few whippings and oatmeal dinners. I resented Yasmine, but I never treated her mean because she was so young. She would do something wrong, and nothing would come of it. She never got what she actually did deserve.

I was in my room one day on a punishment for something unknown, as always. I was sitting on the side in the corner where my daybed was. Yasmine was getting potty trained at the time. She had been made to sit there for a long period of time that day. She got bored. She ended up pooping in her potty chair and began to take the hard feces' out and throw them at me.

She didn't get in any trouble after I called Mrs. Robinson into the room and made her aware of the situation. I did get in trouble. Mrs. Robinson made me stand up in front of the bedroom door with both hands on my head stating I had turned around out of my corner I was placed in. Of course I had only turned around because feces were being thrown at me; but of course, to her, it was punishable.

There were times that Mrs. Robinson would leave and have Fancy watch us. We loved those times of peacefulness in the home. Fancy would let us watch TV, even the PG or PG-13 movies. Her favorite show was Wwe wrestling. That's all we would watch on the designated days and times it came on. We all grew to love it as well and developed our own favorite wrestlers.

The Robinsons did not allow us to watch TV when they were at home. There would be a few times where we would be allowed to watch a program or a movie in their bedroom with them. The most we could do when we weren't on some type of punishment was to read books, sitting in our room or on the steps that led to the basement. When we were left with Fancy, she would break Mrs. Robinsons routine and allow us to be children and enjoy ourselves.

Fancy was a girl who'd had a pretty crappy life as well. She had come to Grand Rapids from Flint, Michigan, a city, which, at one point and time, was the murder capital. She was taken in by the Robinsons because she had no family, and her mom was no good as well. She did grow up with her mom, in contrast to me and my brother. She was around nineteen years old when the Robinsons opened up their home to her.

One thing I precisely remember about Fancy is that she loved her hair. She wore a different wig or weaves all the time and got dressed up even if she wasn't going anywhere. She had a guy friend that would come over all the time and visit her. He was really nice and friendly but not too attractive. He would attend church with us and join us for dinner and such. They were together for a while until Mrs. Robinsons broke them up.

I say Mrs. Robinson broke them up because she always meddled in their business. She was saying bad things about him to Fancy and getting into her head, convincing her to give up on him. Her goal was to control us and her, and she eventually won Fancy's mind.

Fancy was falling prey to Mrs. Robinson more and more each day. Mrs. Robinson began to mistreat her as if she was a child and chastise her when she didn't chastise us. Fancy gradually became a mini–Mrs. Robinson. She was afraid of being homeless and was willing to do whatever was asked of her so she could keep a roof over her head.

Fancy became a monster slowly. Instead of her being an adult and reporting what was going in the home, she joined the cult. Once she started her rampage, she did not know how to stop. She began to act just like Mrs. Robinson, but only when Mrs. Robinson was around.

She still did not do as much as she used to when Mrs. Robinson was gone, and she was left to watch us. I think she feared Mrs. Robinson coming home early and catching her being nice and flipping out on her. Fancy was always in the house with us; she was like an in-home slave. She rarely ever got out; neither did we.

The "every now and then" that we did leave the house, we were still mistreated. On times when we would go to the grocery stores, the Robinsons would leave us all in the car while they did their shopping. We could be in the car for an hour or two, depending on the size of the store and how much food they were getting. Of course we could get out once they got to the van because they wanted us to put the groceries in the car. We were little slaves and servants to them.

It's too bad that our "masta," Mrs. Robinson, was the exact same complexion as we were. Not to mention, every time they would go out to eat, we were always left in the car to make ourselves a sandwich—just like a "masta" feeding his slaves scraps and leftovers or nothing. She would buy some bread and bologna, and her and Mr. Robinson would go in a restaurant and eat while we set in a hot car and ate. She would enjoy five star, and we would enjoy dry sandwiches with just meat and bread.

Now let me say that every now and then, she did have heart. We would be taken to Old Country Buffet quite a bit. It seemed like that was her favorite restaurant, probably because the prices were low. We also went to Ryan's, also known as Fire Mountain now, quite often. These restaurants were our Sunday outings after church.

So sometimes, when she was in a decent mood, she did treat us as her kids and not her slaves, allowing us to get out in public and eat with her and her husband. Most times we were allowed to eat what we wanted, so that was exciting for us since we never go to choose anything at home. We would take full advantage of those days.

She also cooked exceptionally well. She knew how to bake any dessert you could think of—banana bread, zucchini bread, peach cobbler, German chocolate cake, the list goes on. Everything she made was from scratch. She was very skilled in the kitchen. She could also cook anything you would consider soul food.

On the days she felt like making a feast, she would have foods prepared as if we were having company over. The problem was, she was selfish with her food toward us. She'd make the big feast with enough food to feed two families and make us eat the "oatmeal delight" or a sandwich for dinner.

We were always eating something plain or nasty. She, Mr. Robinson, and Fancy would sit and enjoy some ribs, steak, or spaghetti dinner while we watched and drooled. She didn't give us any juice or water. A lot of times we would try to sneak it out the sink. We all were caught every time, so some of the other kids moved to drinking out the toilet. Not fair, huh? I know.

Mrs. Robinson was all about showing out to get attention from everyone. There was a picture she painted of herself as the most loving mom. She felt good and was adored for taking on two different woman responsibilities. It was only natural for her to act as if she was holier-than-thou. She would put the fanciest clothes on us on Sundays and take us to church.

She always wore the most expensive church suits with expensive hats and pairs of shoes to match them. Everyone would talk about how good, cute, smart, and well-mannered we were. Funny, if only they knew the reason we acted like controlled robots. We were not allowed to look at each other in church or talk or move too much; if we did, we would feel a tight grip on our thigh (a pinch) or a twist of our ear.

We went to a church owned by Mr. Robinson's nephew. It was called Greater Harvest Church of God in Christ. I absolutely loved that church. I would be excited to be woken up early on Sunday mornings to attend that church. The church families were so nice and accepting of us. They all knew how to sing exceptionally well.

I loved to sing, so that was my favorite part of service. Going to that church on Sundays was a great escape. We had a lot of young cousins that went there, us girls would look through each other's little pearly white purses and wear our little white gloves, and the boys would horseplay with each other before and after church. It was nice to be away from the house and around other people. At least then, we didn't have to worry about being tortured.

Mrs. Robinson was the true definition of a hypocrite. She used religion to torture us and scare us. A lot of days after coming home from school, she would immediately make us read a specific scripture from the Bible. Now there's nothing wrong with reading the Bible; every kid should be taught to read the Word. That's the one of the best investments you could make for your child.

When you're made to read the Bible all day with no food and you're told you had till the end of the night to have a whole scripture memorized, that's just mean and foul: an eight- or nine-year-old memorizing a complete scripture of which he/she better not miss or add any words or face being punished? Horrible, mean, and dang near impossible. We would be given scriptures like Psalms 91 and Genesis 1 and all the last four chapters of Psalms. That's a lot.

If you did miss any words or added any words you were to be punished, and you were to study that scripture until you literally had every word memorized. You could be on punishment for days because of her ridiculous expectation. When I wasn't made to read the Bible, I was made to read a children's Christian book with short stories in them called "Keys for Kids."

Those stories were at least three paragraphs long with a separate paragraph of topic questions. We were made to memorize the story and the questionnaire as well. Same rules and punishment applied if you missed something out of that book. We were bound to miss something every time because we were only kids. Our memories had not developed fully. I stayed in some type of trouble for forgetting a line or two.

As if the previous requirement wasn't ridiculous enough, she came up with another torture technique. Almost daily, we began to get to on our hands and knees after school and pray all evening. We would be allowed to get up only to pee and eat and would be forced to go back to our knees until bedtime. That was the most pain ever.

We were children, and children's bones and muscles tend to be a little more enduring, but we still experienced pain, being on our knees for hours while reaching all the way up on a dining room chair with our arms up and hands folded was extremely painful. Mrs. Robinson ensured we prayed out loud to make sure that we didn't fall asleep.

Our tender bones ached so badly, and our stomach felt so worked out. When were finally allowed to be up, we could barely move. We would all rush up the steps to lie down in our beds and escape through our sleep and dreams. I could still feel my pain through my sleep. I wondered if there were little kid angels watching over us at night.

At one point and time, Mrs. Robinson took her force of religion to the extreme. She had decided it was time for us to get the Holy Ghost. She had been ranting and raving about demons walking through the house and that the two-year-old boy had a demon in him. She would use these stories to terrify us.

For about a straight week or two, we were on our knees, praying, kneeling on her bed, on our dining room chairs, at our bed for hours, repeating the same chant or prayer. I grew tired of this routine, so I gave up. I decided I was going to act out what I saw the older women doing in church. I wriggled around a little bit, spoke a made-up language, and acted crazy. She just knew I had received the Holy Ghost into me that night. I had gotten the Holy Ghost that day, in my own way.

My brother supposedly caught the Holy Ghost the same night, right after me. We were praised and congratulated for our progress and finally allowed to go bed. It felt so good lying in that bed; my body was so sore, and I was exhausted. The next morning, my brother woke up speaking in tongues; I did not. I didn't know I had to act like this every day every minute of the day.

My adoptive mom was horrified; my brother woke up still speaking in tongues, and I woke up saying good morning. She knew instantly I had faked my catching of the Holy Spirit. She said that if I really had it, I would've woken up speaking the same language I went to bed speaking.

Man did I get it. I was snatched up, yelled at, and knocked back down on my knees. I was made to pray the same prayer for hours past the midnight hour. I was also served the "oatmeal delight" for that night with nothing to drink. So after praying for so long with no water and barley, any food I got thirsty and was hungry.

I had been defeated; by the end of the night, I was in tears. It didn't just end there. I was also whooped for the incident and was whooped dang near every day for several days. Mrs. Robinson said that what I had done was very serious, and I could go to hell for my actions. I never caught the Holy Ghost.

CHAPTER 4

Time went on, and so did my birthdays. There were no celebrations, no presents, no "just this once" good birthday. Birthdays were no special than any other day. I only remember getting one gift one time: a pretty little Indian doll, which I thought was the prettiest doll in the world. I was allowed to play with her for that one day since it was my birthday.

Before I went to bed that night, my doll was taken from me, and I barely saw her again. It was a temporary sense of happiness that was snatched from me as soon as I felt it. Mrs. Robinson would let me get my doll from time to time after that. My doll was like my best friend.

I would play with hair and put lotion in it to make her smell good; she was my joy. She bought me one more doll after that. She was called a Walking Wendy Doll. I would hold Wendy's hand and walk with her around my room. She and the Indian doll were sisters.

Christmas, although considered the ultimate holiday, was no different in this household. There would be a bunch of toys bought, and they would put them in a garbage bag instead of wrapping them. She would let us play with the toys until the end of the night; that would be our last time playing with them for a while. Every now and then, we might get lucky and be allowed to play with the toys. Usually, after the first few nights, the toys would be placed on display shelves.

When people would come over the house, she would brag about what she had bought us to make herself look like a good parent. She would do the same thing with clothes. She would buy a bunch of cute outfits and hang them up in our closet. We would never be allowed to wear them when we wanted to or wear them to school. By the time she was ready for us to show the outfits off, they would be too small for us because she barely took us anywhere; she'd just wind up wasting "our" money.

As the years continued, the abuse got worse and became more in-depth. There was one instance where my brother had done something wrong. I'm not sure what it was that he'd done, but Fancy was made to punish him. Fancy grabbed a big, thick black leather belt and proceeded to whip him. A couple of minutes after the lashing began, blood started to splatter all over the walls and floor, causing everyone to be shocked and fearful.

Fancy had whipped him so hard she had caused his legs to whelp, and the repeated lashes opened the whelps up, causing them to bleed. He had marks all over the bottom half of his body. Fancy finally slowed down and noticed what she had done. She began crying and apologizing repeatedly while trying to stop the blood from falling.

There was a situation where I had gotten into some trouble and was placed on punishment. I was made to sit in the corner the whole day. I'm not sure what I had done. I was always in trouble for something but never knew what it was. Generally it was always something petty, so I'm pretty sure it was for something petty this time around. This particular day, I was made to sit at the top of our basement stairs in the corner.

I was supposed to be waiting for my "oatmeal delight" dinner to be made and served. I had sat there so long I had to use the restroom eventually. I told Mrs. Robinson I had to pee. She told me I had to wait until she was ready to let me go. I waited a few moments and my bladder became fuller. I couldn't take it anymore. I asked to go again; she again replied no. Eventually, I gave up after asking a few more times.

After about a half hour, I could no longer hold it in; I peed on myself. Once I told my Mrs. Robinson I had peed myself, it was on. I was hit, snatched by my hair, and dragged down two flights of steps. I was thrown up against the basement refrigerator, bent over butt naked, and beat with that big, thick black leather belt that was used on my brother.

I was beaten so hard and so long that there were whelps on me and the freezer door. She then told me to go clean my pee and go sit down where I was with my wet clothes on. As if it was my fault that I peed myself, her actions made no sense.

Another punishment I remember was being made to sit in the garage on a crate. I and my brother were on punishment for some reason, and we both were put in the garage. We were made to sit on some cartons with our backs against each other. Instead of being allowed into the house to use the restroom, there was a bucket placed on the side of us.

We were to pee and have our bowel movements in this bucket. Now I don't know what we could possibly have done so bad that we were treated like animals. Matter of fact, there is nothing we could have done that bad that justifies the severity of that punishment.

There were a lot of nights I would just sit and cry wondering why I was living this life. I would always end up crying myself to sleep, wondering when my mom was going to come and rescue me. She never did. There were nights I would just close my eyes and imagine being in my mom's arm. I would try to dream of her and the potlucks at the agency. I kept my vision alive and vivid of her big pregnant belly the day she held me up to the fountain. Her face became faint in my memory of her, but her hair fiasco stayed fresh in my mind.

Mrs. Robinson grew a larger sense of comfort ability with her irrational methods of punishment. She began to misuse and abuse the other kids as well. It had been about a year after they were taken in that she decided it was time to break them in and downright along with us. The youngest boy got tired of her hitting him; he'd had enough.

So one day after she finished yelling at him, he shouted out some profanity toward her. Mrs. Robinson could not believe her ears; we children were cracking up, looking at her facial expression. She snatched his little bony butt up so fast and began to viciously whip him. That small young boy retaliated and fought her back. We were so proud of him!

From that day forward, Mrs. Robinson began engraving in our mind that he was really a demon child. She would treat him horribly. He was always being hit or on some type of a punishment. All the punishments I've mentioned, he got them. On this one particular day, Mrs. Robinson decided to make him go outside on the deck and stand with his hands on his head so she could keep an eye on him. She was outside relaxing in her lounge chair and wanted to make sure he didn't put his arms down.

It was summertime, and the sun was out and shining strong that day. It was about ninety-eight degrees outside on the outdoor patio; there was no form of shade out there to block the sun from beaming down. She had not given him any food or drink since he'd gotten up that morning.

Approximately an hour or so later, Mrs. Robinson, Fancy, and Mr. Robinson came running into the house, screaming and yelling. They burst into my room with Mrs. Robinson screaming for Fancy to call an ambulance. They dropped a small limp body onto my bed. My little brother had become overheated and fainted.

An ambulance made it to our home about fifteen to twenty minutes after the call was placed. The EMS medics rushed into my room checking for his pulse and vitals. They carried his small limp body out the house and to the med bus. He was rushed to the local hospital. Fancy was left to watch over us other four children while the Robinsons rushed to the ER with my brother. The next day, we were picked up from the house and taken to the hospital to see him.

The diagnosis for my little brother was severe case of dehydration. The Robinsons were told by the overseeing physician that their son had been severely dehydrated, and it looked as if he had not had anything to eat or drink in days. He lay in the hospital bed so limp and fragile with an IV stuck up his arm, giving him the electrolytes necessary for him to regain his strength. They were also notified that CPS had been called and made aware of the situation because they had found severe bruising and marks all over his entire body.

CPS showed up at the hospital during our visit with him. They questioned the Robinsons about the scars and bruises that tatted his body. The Robinsons lied and told the worker that the wounds were made from his previous family. They told the worker that they had just adopted him, and a lot of the markings were old; the new ones, she claimed, were made by me.

At this time, I was only eight years old. The doctors and CPS stated there was no way a child could make bruises so deep on another child. They said I was too small, and there was no way my hand was heavy enough to leave a bruise. Mrs. Robinson forced all the kids, including me, to say I caused the marks on his body.

The state still questioned the situation for a while. For a good couple of months, the state continued to come around our home. Since we were all terrified of Mrs. Robinson, we kept our mouths shut. After so much probing and prodding with no feedback from us, the state decided to let it go.

During their investigation, however, we were treated so much better than the norm we'd grown use too. We were going outside every day and riding bikes with our cousins from church. She even let us stay the night with them quite a few times. Things were good for the moment and that moment only.

About a year after the hospital event, my little sister was able to go to school. She was to turn four years old a couple of weeks after school began. She was heading into her preschool year. We were all going to school together except my youngest brother. I believe my youngest brother was going to a head start school since he was he would be turning three in October.

My little sister's looks must have started to fade out in Mrs. Robinsons eyes because she began to abuse Yasmine as well. Yasmine went to school with black blisters on the back of her hands all the time from the spatula punishment.

One day, while Yasmine was playing on some monkey bars at school, a teacher noticed some blisters on her knuckles and asked her what had happened. CPS was called back out to the house once again. The Robinsons were questioned about the dark swelling on the backs of her hands.

Mrs. Robinson came up with a story saying Yasmine had accidentally slammed her fingers in the car door. This time they decided that the story was not going to be acceptable. The state became involved in the Robinsons' home affairs again. They decided to keep tabs on the Robinsons for a little while longer this time around.

Once again, the facade was used to cover up everything real and true. We were playing outside living the average kids' lives. One of our older family members that were kin to Mr. Robinson moved next door with her son. She was a sweet lady that would always invite me over to hang out with her.

She was like a stepmom to me. She gave me more one time and attention than my adoptive mom. I was allowed to go over her house all the time. I was able to eat normal food, drink juice, and run around the house, something I was not used too. Her home was my "home away from house."

We had another family that moved in on the other side of us, the Mibers. The Mibers were a couple who were probably a little younger than the Robinsons. The Mibers had two older children, both were boys. We began going over her home all the time. Mrs. Miber was the sweetest woman ever. She would give us snacks after school and let us watch TV at her home.

A lot of times we would get home from school, and the Robinsons would not be at the house. We would just sit on our front porch and wait. If Mrs. Miber made it home before Mr. and Mrs. Robinson, we would go sit in Mrs. Miber's house with her kids. She would help all five of us with our homework then we'd watch cartoons on TV. When the Robinsons came home, they would come knock at their door and tell us to come home.

Time went by and the state dropped the case yet again. We still had not opened our mouths to tell anything. The state decided they couldn't get anything solid enough on the Robinsons. We were once again left prey to the wild woman on the hunt for blood. I was once again put back into my corner in the attic every day.

At one point in time, I was on punishment in that corner for an entire week. One day, after coming home, Mrs. Robinson went into the attic and grabbed her church suit off the hooks (she was picking out her Sunday outfit) that hung in the little hallway leading to the steps. She went into her room with her outfit to set out her Sunday clothes. A few minutes later, all I could hear was Mrs. Robinson screaming and ranting. She was carrying on like a chicken with its head cut off.

She called all the kids into the hallway and began to interrogate each of us. Her church suit had gotten a small snag in it somehow. She was screaming and yelling, trying to figure out who'd caused the small rip. Everyone stated they had not touched her outfit. It had been covered with the cleaner's plastic the entire time it hung there.

Everyone else was turned loose and sent back to bed except me. She asked me again if I did do it. I told her I had not. Why would I do more to get a worse or longer punishment? She still did not believe a word I said. She began elaborating on the fact that I was the only one who was in the attic all the time. How could she really know when it happened and who did it? Fancy's room was the attic, so what about her?

After questioning me for several minutes, Mrs. Robinson became convinced it was me that messed up her outfit. She was starting to scare me to death. I didn't know what she was going to do to me. She had so much evil in her eyes; smoke was coming out her nostrils. She told me if I'd just tell the truth I wouldn't have to be punished as bad as I was if I kept supposedly lying.

She told me that if I kept lying, it was going to be horrible for me at the end of it all. I broke down and lied on myself. I told her yes, I ripped the suit jacket. She then began questioning me how I had done it. I told her I used a bobby pin to cut the jacket. She got mad at me all over again and told me I had to have used scissors because the rip was precise and straight-edged. I didn't even know where the scissors were in the house.

Mrs. Robinson snatched me down those three attic steps so quick I barely had time to blink. There were three steps that led to a little platform and then more steps that led to the attic upstairs. I had went back to stand on the platform in the attic corner. She grabbed a big handful of hair and dragged me from the hallway of the attic down the main hallway and threw me into the bathroom.

She then entered the bathroom, hitting me all over my body with her hands and a belt. She instructed Fancy to grab her some scissors out of the kitchen. I had no idea if she was about to cut me or the suit up out of anger. She cut my hair off. She took a big hand-ful of my hair and cut whichever way while jerking my head all over.

At that time, my hair had already grown back from the crap my previous foster mom's niece had done. So my hair had been hanging long and thick down my back. My hair was gone again; tears poured out my eyes as I watched my long hair fall into a pile on the bath-room floor. She told me that since I had cut the thing, how did I feel about my hair being cut?

Mrs. Robinson's rampage had only just begun; she continued the scene out into the hallway. She threw me on the floor and instructed Fancy to grab her one of our big, cheap plastic baseball bats. She grabbed the bat and begins to beat me with it. I struggled to try and get away from her. I twisted and turned, trying to get out of her grip.

She woke my older brother up and made him sit on my back near the top of my head. Mr. Robinson was told to hold my feet and Fancy was holding my arms down. By this time, I was completely exposed in the nude. She took the giant plastic bat and whipped me with it for a good few minutes.

I wiggled out of Fancy's grip and ended up turning my head; the bat hit me straight in the eye! I was finally let up from the defeated wrestler position and released to my room. My eye was aching and so was the whole back of my body. That didn't put a stop to her craziness; she came in my room periodically, the entire night, and woke me out my sleep, beating me with a belt. I woke up the next morning with a black eye and was kept home from school for a week until my eyelids returned to their appropriate color.

CHAPTER 5

Since Mrs. Robinson had a problem keeping her hands to herself and did not want to get caught up, again, she moved me to a different school. This was a big school in a nicer community. I liked it a lot. It was full of nice, intelligent kids, and the inside of the school and surroundings were more kid-friendly than my previous school. I had a great teacher, but I still had no friends. I didn't know how to make friends, and if I did, I could never visit or socialize with them outside of school, so I kept to myself. I was what someone would call antisocial.

By the time I was placed into this school, I was ten years old and in the fifth grade. I had a female teacher that I really admired and adored. It was a joy being in her class, and she was always making us read new and exciting books then have class projects on them. English was my favorite subject; I loved to read, and English still is my fave.

So anything that had to do with reading and writing was exciting to me so I loved her class. I thrived for more readings and soaked up everything I read, imagining the picture to the story. I wished reading and writing was the subject of my class all day. Reading was a great escape from my home life. Whenever I was able to sit down and made to read a book at home, I imagined the pictures that went with the story, and I would become a bystander in the story.

Our midyear class trip was coming up. We were going to take a trip to Mackinac Island, in Mackinaw City, Michigan. I had a strong feeling that I would not be going. The field trip was $40, and a woman who would only buy me thrift store clothes wasn't likely to pay my fee.

My teacher noticed that I was wearing the same clothes every day and my spirit was down, so she offered to pay my way. She told me I still needed my permission slip signed by my parents. I hung my head down and reluctantly replied okay. When I told Mrs. Robinson, she said she would sign it.

I could go! I was so excited! I could not wait. She never signed the slip. The day of the trip, my teacher called my home. She told my adoptive parents she would pick me up and take me to school to board the bus for the trip. Mrs. Robinson told her no, I was asleep, and I was not going. I was so hurt.

A lot of schools have a spokesperson come in and speak with children about "red flag" and "green flag." We had one of those people come into our class and go over the do's and don'ts. At the end of the lecture, the speaker asked if anyone had questions or knew someone who was being hit on. I raised my hand and answered yes to the question about being abused. I was sent to the office to speak with the principal. I told the principal everything, and he called my adoptive mom and told her everything. She told the principal I was a habitual liar, and she would talk to me about it when we got home.

When we got out the van, I thought I was good to go. I was dead wrong. As soon as we made in into the house, I went upstairs and was called right back down. As I made it to the last step, I was punched in the chest by Mrs. Robinson. She knocked the wind out of me; not to mention, she knocked me to the ground.

She yelled at me, saying I was to go to school and tell the school I made up the whole thing. Later on that night, I was stomped repeatedly—literally stepped on and pounced on for several seconds. Mrs. Robinson was a big woman; I'm surprised nothing broke in me.

Fancy got sick of the constant bull all the time. Mrs. Robinson had snatched her up by her neck one day and threatened her for one reason or another. Fancy started leaving out the house more often by herself. She found her a man and began dating again. She winded up falling in love. She moved out of the "house of horrors" and got married. Mrs. Robinson wasn't too thrilled about her decision, but there was nothing she could do; Fancy was a grown woman. Mrs. Robinson was ready to move out of Grand Rapids; she decided to move to Kalamazoo.

The state had got involved in our home again after my incident at school had been reported to CPS. Our assigned worker had filed for a court-signed petition stating that the Robinsons were not to leave the city with a pending investigation of abuse allegations.

The Robinsons were extremely upset and aggravated. They had cleaned the entire house and packed up everything in the home. On top of that, they had already terminated their lease. We moved in with our neighbors, the Mibers. Mrs. Robinson prayed and hoped the hold would be lifted so we could move soon.

For several months, we lived a normal life because of our move in with the Mibers. Mrs. Robinson was not crazy enough to engage in abusing us in another family's home, let alone in front of others. She kept her meanness to a minimum; she would attempt some things when the Mibers were gone about their business, running errands and such.

Overall, we were safe and free for once. It felt pleasantly good and refreshing. We went to Vacation Bible School that summer; afterward, we would come home and Mrs. Miber would serve snacks with some milk. I felt like I was living the life. We'd watch TV and cartoons all the time and would play outside. All of us kids would sit around at night and talk about how we wished the Mibers could be our parents.

Approximately three to four months later, they lifted the hold off the move. The Robinsons were free to move us to Kalamazoo, Michigan. There was one small but vital stipulation: the only way they could go was if the state assigned someone to oversee and check in on us every now and then.

Once we moved, the Robinsons were ordered to put us into counseling as well. I believe they did this thinking they could manipulate us into opening up our mouths about the abuse. The best way for them to do this is to get a soft-talking stranger with skills to make us spill our guts.

The Robinsons got a beautiful home. It was a two-story home with five bedrooms, two kitchens, two living rooms, two dining rooms, three bathrooms, and a large master bedroom with a bathroom the size of a large bedroom with a hotel-sized Jacuzzi tub. There was a walk-in closet the size of one of our rooms.

It was a huge home with a large kitchen with marble countertops and marble floors to match. It had a two-stall garage, which was needed because by this time, the Robinsons had purchased a small Daewoo. They now had three vehicles, an Expedition, a Daewoo, and a Lincoln town car.

We were so brainwashed that therapy still did not work. We went to our meetings, but we still did not say much. The therapist figured everyone was too anti-social, so they suggested the Robinsons enrolled us into a summer program. We went there once a week taking the bus sometimes and getting rides the other times. By this time, we were all above the age of five, so me and my older brother were the lookouts for the younger siblings.

We would have fun at this place. They had basketball in one room, art class in another. There were a bunch of rooms in which there were different activities to engage in. We were finally out the house; off the steps we were always made to sit and read on all day. We saw sunshine, weird people, and other kids. We were having fun. Life had changed so much. The abuse was still going on, but it was less often and not as severe.

We continued our visits with the therapist and hung out. Our home life was still boring. We sat on the steps all day reading books or the Bible. We still were not allowed to watch TV, only on special occasions. We still were yelled and hollered at about everything.

Mrs. Robinson began to pick on the middle-aged boy. She punched him in his back so hard one day just for not putting some cans into the cabinet quick enough. I thought she broke his back, his scream was so loud and high-pitched it sounded like he was dying.

My school there was much worse. We lived in a mainly white neighborhood with a few black families. Some of whom were Mrs. Robinson kin. She had a brother at one end, and I believe a cousin at the other end that was closer to us. I went to middle school with some mean children who would use racist and demeaning words toward me and my brother almost every day on the bus. We never tried to fight them; we just ignored it and told our adoptive parents.

I got teased the most at school because of certain things concerning my physical appearance. I was twelve and a half years old with no boobs and a five o'clock shadow above my lips which I made worse by putting tape on it and leaving it overnight. I woke up the next morning with red above my lip that turned blacker with time.

I was told and saw that most girls my age had breasts or were growing them. I came home so many days just crying with my feelings hurt. When I did begin to grow my nipples, Mrs. Robinson refused to buy me a bra. I walked around with my big nipples showing through all my shirts and getting teased for a couple of months until my therapist told her it was time for me to have one.

To add fuel to the fire, it didn't help that I had the biggest crush ever on a guy that didn't like me. I thought he was the cutest boy in the school, and he was one of the ones teasing me. I soon began to grow breast fat behind my nipples, forming my small breasts. They never quite grew past that point.

I was teased, and rumors were spreading that I was stuffing my bra. So first, I'm teased for being flat, and then I was teased for having big nipples, now I was growing breasts and accused of stuffing. I couldn't win for losing.

I went home early plenty of times. I was always crying and depressed in school. I was tired of being teased, and the kids weren't letting up. I stayed with a stomachache due to nervousness and anxiety every time I left for school. Mrs. Robinson would let me come home early. Of course she would make me walk home, but she would be so nice to me at these times.

She'd tell me I was just a late developer, and I was going to grow to be beautiful and developed. The beautiful part is true, developing my boobs, not quite. I felt so close to her at these times, my sad moments due to the treatment of others was when I was treated like her daughter.

Every morning, we were made to clean up the downstairs kitchen and make up our beds. Every now and then, if Mrs. Robinson was up this early, she would come downstairs and go over everything with a fine-tooth comb. If anything was out of place, she would make the mess bigger than what it was and make us re-clean the whole entire area.

If the bed had one wrinkle, she would pull the comforter and sheets back and make us remake the bed again. One dish with a spot, all the dishes would go back in the sink to be washed. Nothing was ever done to her satisfaction. She made us miss our bus plenty of times and would make us walk if she did.

I got my first official haircut at thirteen years old. My adoptive mom's pastor owned a beauty shop. She paid him to cut my hair even and into a style. She dropped me off at the shop and told me to tell him to give me a bob. When I came out the shop, I had a bang above my eyes, and my hair was at a mid-ear length.

I wanted to cry. My hair had just grown back from Mrs. Robinson's last antic; now it was gone again. I don't know if Mrs. Robinson didn't know what a bob was, but she was piping hot mad. She said she told him a bob, but she didn't want it that short. She asked why I didn't tell him to stop cutting, I didn't know about bobs. She told me to tell him a bob, and I assumed he knew what length to cut it since they had previously discussed him being in my head.

CHAPTER 6

One of Mrs. Robinson's family members down the street had three foster children. We were allowed to play with them and stay nights every now and then. Those were good times. We all use to ride our bikes together through the trails around the area and down the big steep street we stayed on.

I tried to ride my bike with no hands and turn the corner going down the steep street. Dumbest mistake I ever made. I flew off the bike and hit the ground, bumping my head and scraping up my elbows and both knees. I messed up our evening; we all had to go inside because of my stupidity.

By this time my adoptive father had endured two strokes. By the grace of God, that man could still walk, talk, and function on his own. Out of two full strokes, he only developed a stuttering issue and was a little weak-minded. Mrs. Robinson used this to her fullest advantage.

She yelled and screamed at him all the time. She wanted him to discipline us more. She said he always made her out to be the heavy, and it was time he intervened. Feeling pressured and not being completely in his right frame of mind, he began to become mean and slightly abusive. Every now and then, he would hit or put us on punishment. This was not very often; he was a very sweet man, just a little confused and easily persuaded.

My brother used to lay in his bed and cry every night. He was just so unhappy and all the years of pain had got to him. He was older, fourteen years old, and understanding, realizing our life was not right. One night, he and my adoptive father got into a fight.

My adoptive dad hit my brother with a big plastic showcase guitar that hung on the basement wall. My brother snatched it out his hand and tried to hit him back. Mrs. Robinson intervened and took the guitar from my brother and sent him to bed. The next morning, my brother was gone. He had snuck out the basement window in his room.

Months went by, and I still did not see my brother. I had no idea where he was or if he was okay. Things became tense at home. We were made to do everything. We cleaned up everything, made the Robinsons' bed, Mrs. Robinson even made us put her shoes on. I would always be sick from using ammonia and bleach to scrub the patch of cream carpet in front of the upstairs bathroom.

Mrs. Robinson begun to pick on me again. She teased me one day about my small boobs. I was humiliated that she would hit me so low below the belt; I began to cry and ran out the back door. I called myself running away but had nowhere to go.

I just walked all over our side of town looking for the one and only friend I had—home. She wasn't there, so I left and walked back home. By the time I made it back home, Mrs. Robinson had called her sister-in-law down the street. She had a little one-on-one speech with me about the dangers of my behavior.

About three months after my brother's disappearance, we came home to a message on the answering machine. It was a message left by the worker who was overseeing our case. He stated that we would be getting picked up later on that afternoon.

Mrs. Robinson was to pack us a bag with enough clothes for a week or two. Mrs. Robinson began to cry, and so did we. We had no idea where we were going and after eight years of being with someone, good or bad, you become attached and used to a certain person or situation. We were terrified!

A couple of hours after hearing the message, the worker arrived at the home. The police sat outside the home. They were there to ensure that our removal went smoothly. The worker entered the back door off the garage and came into the kitchen to talk to everyone about what was going on. He explained that there had been some allegations made against the Robinsons. Since this was a recurring event, we had to be removed so they could fully investigate.

I think that was the wisest decision they'd made for once. Get us out of the devil's sight so that we could feel comfortable and finally let everything be known. After grabbing our bags and allowing us to say good-bye, we were led outside to the worker's car. I sat in front and the younger children were put in the back of the vehicle. That was last time I saw the Robinsons as a child.

We were in the car for about twenty minutes until we reached the other side of town. We were now in the hood. There were people everywhere. Groups of men hung out on every corner, at the corner store, and on every front porch in the neighborhood. I was scared of my surroundings. I had went to school in a community like this before, but it had been a while, and I was uncomfortable.

I was hoping we were just passing through the area, but I was sadly mistaken when the worker turned down one of the streets near the corner store. He stopped at an old off-white house sitting on the corner. He told us that this is where we would be staying for a while until they figured out the best choice for us. He assured us it was just a temporary placement, and he would be working on our case.

Now I love the foster mom to death that I'm going to be discussing. However I'm going to keep it real. Everything I saw and felt will be discussed in full detail, no holding back. We all exited the vehicle including the worker and headed up the steps to the front door. The worker knocked on the front door of the screened in porch. A woman answered and began to speak with the worker. After introducing us to her and making sure everyone was okay, he left, reassuring us he'd be back in a few weeks.

We all walked into the home together like Siamese twins. We looked around, unsure of what to do. It was very basic house — old cloth furniture in a junky living room, messy kitchen; it was an average lived-in home. I was instantly upset and disgusted; my previous house looked like a magazine picture out of *Good Housekeeping*. This setup had nothing on our house. I did not want to live there even if it was temporary.

My new foster mom, Ms. Karen, led us up the steps to our room. The upstairs had a very nice bathroom; it was a large bathroom with the biggest tub I'd ever seen. That bathroom was definitely cooler than the rest of the house. It was a very large bedroom next to it, with two beds in it. We girls were to sleep in one bed, and the boys were to sleep in the other bed. Ms. Karen also had two boys of her own that slept in a room across the hall from us.

I put my bags down next to our assigned bed and sat down. The younger kids followed suit. Words cannot explain the way I felt at that very moment. I just could not believe all this stuff had happened to me. Why? Ms. Karen saw the sad looks on all of our faces and began to comfort us. She was a very sweet woman. She calmly explained what was going on and that it was temporary—the same thing the worker told us. That didn't change our demeanor. We were still scared and upset.

Not too long after, Ms. Karen left the room, so did we. We went downstairs and sat on the couch and watched TV. A couple of days went by and we continued to sit around on the couch everyday just watching TV. This new mom didn't complain or make us do anything. All we were asked to do was keep our room clean and our beds made. She never raised her voice; she was so pleasant to be around.

Ms. Karen was tired of seeing us sitting around depressed. She suggested that we go outside and play, meet some new people, make friends. We took her advice and did just that. We went outside every day from that point on. We had never been allowed to just get up and go outside with that much ease.

All we had to do now was tell her we were going out, and that was the end of it, she'd say okay, stay in the area. So we could watch TV when we wanted and go outside when we pleased? Wow! We were living the life! We never wanted this sense of happiness to end.

A few days before our worker was to come talk to us, I gathered my brother and sisters for a family meeting. I discussed how well we were being treated and that we should stay here forever. I encouraged everyone to tell the worker all that they had experienced with the Robinsons. They all agreed. Why give this up to go back and be beaten and used? So it was settled. We found our new mom, and we were determined to stay.

The worker showed up as promised. He gathered us all and asked how everything was going. After gathering up information from all of us, he then sent us out the room and called us in one by one. He asked questions about the Robinsons and told me my brother had been found.

That's why we had been removed from the home. My brother had told everything. I told him everything as well. The worker looked as if he wanted to cry while I told him some of the vicious punishments I had endured. He wrote everything down furiously in his notebook, looking up at me every now and then. One by one, the rest of the kids told their sides.

Our worker couldn't say for sure, yet although he knew, we weren't going back to the Robinsons. After pulling the Robinsons into court and going over the allegations and evidence gathered against them, it was settled. We were to be removed permanently from the Robinsons home.

The parental rights of both were revoked. They could never again do foster care, adopt, or even keep their birth kid if they had one. Their rights were terminated. They were told to give us the rest of our belongings, but they never did. All my childhood pictures and memories were gone.

CHAPTER 7

It was over! We were free! Our worker called and told us the good news after the hearing. It was such a sense of relief! We all jumped up and down thanking Jesus and crying. As I write this part of the story, I'm swarmed with the same emotions I had that very moment. I have chills running through my body, I remember that day very vividly. I was also allowed to have my original birth name back. I signed that petition immediately. I did not want to be a Robinson longer than I had to.

Months went by, and I became attached and grew to love Ms. Karen. She was the best mom I had ever had. She was gentle, loving, and fair. She treated us just as well as she treated her birth children. We were considered equals in her home. We ate what she ate. We went wherever she went. Sundays we would go to church where I enjoyed the sermon and the atmosphere because I knew I wasn't going to be pinched through-out the entire service.

Ms. Karen didn't seem like she had a lot of money from the looks of her home and her clothing, but she wasn't money hungry. Every month she got our check, she spent it on us. I remember the first time I got some clothes. You would have thought I got some Coogi, Polo, or Roca wear by my reaction.

The clothes were brand new with tags on them. That brand name was enough for me. It was one of the few times I received brand-new clothes and could wear them when I pleased. My outfits were so cute for my age. I jumped up and down, saying thank you repeatedly and hugging my foster mother. That was a good day.

Life at my new home was good and getting better. I was getting use to everything and growing more comfortable with every passing day. I made quite a few friends in the neighborhood. It was summertime, so I just enjoyed going outside to the parks and the corner store I'd previously dreaded.

I would go and buy juice and chips every day I was relaxing. I had a girlfriend down the street around my age that I would go and hang out with often. I was thirteen and being treated like a teenager, being treated my age.

I will admit that I became a little too comfortable with my newfound freedom, and I began to be disobedient. I craved attention from anyone and everyone. After being cooped up in a house for eight years, I wanted to be seen, to be known. I stayed walking around the streets all day every day looking for the wrong type of attention. I was always teased in middle school, and

I just wanted to know that I was beautiful and that my body was nice now that I was older.

For those of you that were thinking, "What type of attention?" I am referring to being "hollered" at and having men shout "Damn, she fine" type of attention. I was not having sex. I knew nothing about sex at this age because I never watched TV or went anywhere growing up. I just walked around pulling my shorts up higher than what was necessary and flirting with every boy around my age. There did wind up one incident where one older guy almost showed me what sex was.

He was an older boy who hung out around the neighborhood. He lived a little further up the block and around the corner. I believe he was around eighteen or nineteen years old. By this time, I was only fourteen. He made it seem as if he liked me and wanted to talk to me about something. He had me sit with him behind an old abandoned house on a picnic bench. He proceeded to talk and spit game at me.

Of course I was confused about what the man was relating to. I have never engaged in any type of sexual activity and was innocent to his advances. When he attempted to convince me into sleeping with him, his action scared me and I told him I did not want to. He got upset, called me out of my name, and I went home.

Ms. Karen was getting tired of my behaviors and attitude. I was breaking curfew dang near every night, and worst of all, I'd become disrespectful and mean. I cared about her feelings, but I couldn't stop. I had never lived; I didn't know how to embrace it and take it slow. So I lived it fast.

I remember when I chased this boy that liked me down the street from my house. He had thrown a rock at me and I was trying to hit him. He took off running, cracking up. I took off after him, running and tripped over the curb and twisted my ankle. He ran away, laughing at me while I sat in pain in the middle of the street holding my ankle. I tried to stand up, but the pain was unbearable. I couldn't put any pressure on my ankle. I hopped home and told Ms. Karen I needed to be taken to the ER.

Ms. Karen took me to the ER. Soon after, a doctor entered the room, asking what had taken place to cause my injury. My foster mother sarcastically replied, "She was running the streets being fast."

I laugh as I type this because she was not lying. The doctor confirmed that my ankle was sprained. He wrapped it up, gave me some crutches, and told me to use them for four to six weeks and follow up with my primary doctor. Ms. Karen told me, "Now you gotta sit yo butt down. Ain't no more running the streets for you for a while." The next morning, I got dressed and left the house. I had to prove her wrong. I had to defy her.

Ms. Karen's son was about two years younger than me but big for his age. He had a cousin who came over almost daily. He and his cousin had a thing for me. I felt the same way about the cousin but not my foster brother. I would flirt with his cousin every time he came over. I was a tease, I must admit.

I flirted but never went any further than that. I guess he and his cousin got tired of seeing me flirt and try to be cute for attention. So they decided to try me, but I wasn't having it. They didn't take that too well.

Now I hate that this will be the first time for Ms. Karen to hear about this day, but it's a significant part of my life. I stated I would be honest and tell all, and I still am going to do that. Since I refused to engage in any sexual activity with him or his cousin, they decided they would get something, anything, by any means necessary.

The house was empty that day. Mrs. Karen had gone somewhere and took my younger siblings with her. The only people in the house were me and her son. I was getting dressed and going to head out for the day. My foster brothers' cousin showed up as I was getting ready to head out. I stopped and made conversation for a minute or two.

They both ended up in the same room and begin to make inappropriate conversation with me. I giggled and told them they were nasty and I was leaving. They then stopped from leaving and turned toward me, saying what they wanted to do "it" to me. I shouted no, I didn't want to. I wasn't ready for that. They didn't give up; they became persistent.

I ran back up the steps and was caught by my legs. They tried to pull me back down the steps, all the while tugging at my buttoned-up shirt trying to pry it apart. I held my shirt tightly and pulled on my shirt upward to keep the buttons from popping open. I wriggled and kicked my legs, trying to get loose.

I did get loose, eventually. I was crying and yelling and ran into my room. I closed the door and pressed my weight up against it, trying to use all my might. But they were both teenage boys who were taller and stronger than I was. They got in, and I ran to the bed. I curled up into a ball, trying my hardest to stay in this position so there was nothing they could touch or mess with.

They pried my arms apart, pulling and grabbing. They got my arms! They put my arms back above my head and held them down with one hand a piece. They pulled my bra up above my small breast and began to bite and suck on them, laughing. When they were done, I laid there crying and feeling nasty and disgusted. I can't count how many times I rubbed and scrubbed and scratched my chest trying to get rid of the feel of their mouths off me.

I never told anyone but God. I couldn't tell Ms. Sharon; she'd think I was fast. If I told her, who was to say she wouldn't think I asked for it, I engaged in it, or I liked it. I didn't want it, and I didn't like it. I felt nasty, embarrassed, shamed, and disgusted with myself and the situation. She would never believe me.

I'd tell and be kicked out because she'd think I was lying about her son. Where would I go then? So I kept my mouth shut and kept moving. I couldn't look at him or at his cousin in the same way anymore. There was always awkwardness among us. I wanted to cry or attack them every time I saw them. I acted as if nothing ever happened. Same as my first foster mom, I got over it.

My attitude and moods grew worse. I was pissed about what had happened, and since I held everything inside, I was bitter. I wasn't happy anymore; I was angry. So I acted out even more. I broke my curfew again and was scolded. I screamed back and yelled at Ms. Karen like I was a grown woman. That was the last straw. I had to go. The worker came the next week or so and removed me from the home. They told me I was going back to Grand Rapids for placement.

CHAPTER 8

Since I was now fourteen years old, the state had a very difficult time finding me a foster home. I was over the age limit that most foster parents were willing to take in. A lot of foster parents fear taking in older kids because they've experienced a bad life a lot longer than a young child.

That posed a threat for more problems and issues. Especially for those that were physically and sexually abused as I was. To top it off, the workers have to tell the new parent everything, including my behavior issues with the last parent. That made it even harder for me to get a home.

I was placed in a short-term residential program called Kids First. They had not found me a foster home in the amount of time they were given to remove me. The group home campus was absolutely beautiful. There were a bunch of homes all over the campus.

They were well decorated with flowers and bushes all around the fronts of them. There were large fields and a basketball court not too far from the administration building. Kids First was set in the front of Saint John's Home furthest away from all the individualized homes I had seen. I was told I'd be here temporarily until they found me a new foster home.

The inside of my home was very basic. The entrance led straight into the main part of the house. Everything was right there. The kitchen was off to the side of the dining room, and the dining room was just behind the living room. There was a cloth sofa and a loveseat, a few big lazy-boy–type chairs with a large bookcase in the living room with a small outdated TV on a stand.

The kitchen was huge with an island in the middle; the dining room had a bunch of circle tables lined up next to each other. There were a lot of chairs around the tables, so I assumed a bunch of kids lived there as well. There were a few kids scattered around—boys and girls sitting on the couches and chairs. They just stared at me as I stood there looking around my new surroundings.

My worker went and talked to a staff member while I waited to be introduced. After introducing me to the staff members and making sure I knew what was going to happen from that point on, my worker left. I was told that she would be in touch and would be working on finding me a new foster home.

The staff member took me to the other side of the home down a long hallway to my room. There were two rooms on each side of the hallway with a bathroom dividing them. My room was the first room to the left. It had a big, heavy wooden door, and the inside of the room was carpeted. There was a small wooden bunk bed and a desk in there.

There were another girl's clothes and shoes on the floor, so I knew I had a roommate. I was told to put my things up and come back out when I was ready. I sat down at the desk and began to cry. After letting my emotions out, I put my things up and left the room to join the other children in the main quarters.

I was called downstairs to talk to the in-home worker. She explained the basics of the program and what was expected of me during my stay. A staff member brought me back upstairs and explained the rules and regulations of the house.

There were so many rules and procedures. I could not just get on the phone and talk to who I wanted. I had to have a phone list of which my lawyer had to approve. I was only allowed to call the people on that list, and there was a time limit on phone usage. There was a certain time of day where we all had to go in our rooms for one hour.

It was called quiet time, as if we were small children. We could either sleep, read a book, or write, but we had to stay in the room. If we needed to come out to use the restroom, we had to knock on their door and wait for someone to answer.

The boys' rooms were on the other side of the home. They had the same setup. Girls were not allowed on that side of the building. I had not yet been introduced to any of the kids because most of them were gone on visits or were outside with some of the other staff members. So I was to be formally introduced to everyone around dinnertime.

There were chores for everyone when it came to mealtimes. There was someone assigned to set the table, to wash dishes, to sweep, to mop, and someone to put the dishes in a dishwasher. There were a lot of kids, so I don't blame them for using this strategy; it made mealtime go by a lot smoother.

I was assigned to a CASA worker before my discharge. A CASA is a court-assigned special advocate. I loved that woman. She was the sweetest old lady ever! She would pick me and take me out to movies and lunch. My brother and I had been reconnected by then, but I really don't recall the reunion. My CASA worker would take us both out sometimes. We were able to spend some time together, and she would take us down to Kalamazoo to see our other siblings. She was their casa as well. We all enjoyed her. She had to be the most kind, unselfish, loving woman.

I was at the placement for about a month or less until they finally found me a foster home. My foster mom came to the agency to meet me and announced I'd be coming to live with her. She was an older woman with some grays, and she smelled like cigarettes. Her name was Viriam. I had never been around smokers, so I hoped I'd grow use to the smell.

She helped me grab my belongings, and I followed her to a green truck. She put my things inside the trunk and told me to hop up front with her. Up front, she had Tweety Bird hanging out on her dashboard. I thought that was pretty cute and young. I asked her the story behind the toy, and she told me she just loved Tweety Bird. We pulled out the parking lot, and I was on my way to see my new home.

We drove for a while and all I heard was rap and R & B. I had heard some R & B music living at my last home but not this much rap. My adoptive mom had allowed us to only listen to gospel, so I knew no names of any artist or any words. My last foster mom listened to some R & B, not rap, so listening to this lady's music had my head going crazy trying to figure out the words. I learned the words real quick.

At last, we arrived outside of a big cream house with a large front yard. She helped me gather my bags from the back, and we headed into the house. The house had a huge living room and dining room and the floors were all wooden. I was to sleep on the couch the first night until she made up a bunk bed in a room next to hers.

That night on the couch was a scary experience. I was in the hood again and in a big living room by myself. I heard little mice running around; I thought I was going to get bitten. I wrapped my sheets tightly around me so no mouse could grab onto my cover and climb up. I slept balled up the entire night. I was determined not to get eaten by one of those rodents. I hated mice ever since I saw the mouse a size of a human.

The next day, I woke up, and Ms. Viriam made me breakfast. We talked as she smoked her cigarette and drunk some coffee. She asked me about the group home and other questions concerning my life. She seemed very nice and interested. After finishing up breakfast, I got dressed, and we headed out. We went to her daughter's home so that I could meet her. I would be watched by her when Ms. Viriam went to work. She worked at Menards as a security guard.

Ms. Viriam's daughter was a big woman with a very deep voice. She seemed pretty nice. She had a quaint apartment with lots of yard space for playing. We sat around her house for a while, talking and watching TV. When everything that needed to be discussed had been brought up and talked about, we left. We ran a few errands and went home. Ms. Viriam's son came over a little later to meet me as well. He was gorgeous— light brown, tall, with pretty light hazel or green eyes. (I kinda forgot the color; they weren't brown though.) I had developed a crush instantly.

Ms. Viriam started back to work after I got settled into the home. I went to her daughter's house every time she worked. I always had fun there. I would play outside with other kids in the area and watch TV with my foster mom's daughter. When Ms. Viriam would arrive, I would look forward to the ride home.

I loved the type of music she played in the truck, and it would be loud. I was adapting to my new home more and more each day. Ms. Viriam was a woman with a potty mouth, and she was pretty hard core. I didn't dare talk to her as I had Ms. Karen. This woman was the definition of "I don't play that."

CHAPTER 9

I started my first year of high school soon after the placement. I was to go to Ottawa Hills High School because we were in the school district. I had no friends there, and I was scared to go by myself. I didn't have a choice. I had my foster mom put some crotchets in my hair; I was teased as soon as I got to school.

Bad move for me; they were out of style already. I had never been too in-style, so I had no idea they weren't popular. I had seen girls with them about a year back; man, does stuff go out of style quickly. I had my foster mom take them down as soon as I got home that day. She made me explain why because she spent a lot of time putting them in. When I explained the teasing I experienced because of them, she wrapped my hair and let it hang around my face instead.

School was horrible. The kids were so mean to me. I was not the best-dressed, and like I said, I had no friends. I was a loner. Everyone else had been friends with each other since elementary school, so there were a lot of cliques formed. No one ever gave me a chance to be their friend or tried to be nice to me because I wasn't in their previous childhood circle.

I was nervous every day I went through those front doors. I would sweat profusely and become musty, so the other kids picked on me because of my body odor. I had never been taught how to correctly clean myself when I was growing up, so I didn't know I wasn't washing properly. I was reliving my middle school years again!

Ms. Viriam explained to me how to wash myself so that I would not experience that discomfort again. She took me shopping at Wal-Mart and bought me a huge amount of clothes. I had new pants, shirts, bras, and panties. I thought my outfits were the cutest, but kids at school still teased me because they weren't brand-named.

I couldn't win for losing. I was cute in some of the boys' eyes, so I made guy friends before I did females. There was one boy who used to walk me home. He was a gentleman. I didn't like him in a boyfriend type of way so we just became close friends.

Since I walked home alone most of the time, I decided it was time to start socializing with others who walked home the same way as me. That's when I met Nangie. She was a few years beyond me in high school, but she didn't make it a big deal. She and I began to walk home together after school. She lived right up the street from me, so it was perfect. On the weekends, I would spend the day at her house hanging out; we'd walk to the corner stores in the area just to have some-thing to do.

I'd finally made a friend, so I grew more comfortable with going to school. I begin to talk a little more at school after becoming Nangie's friend. I grew a sense of confidence. I made a lot of friends after stepping out my box a little more—most of them were male. They all had other female friends, so I'd associate with them as well.

The group of friends I'd selected to be cool with were considered dorks. I was not associated with the popular crowd either, so I still was picked on regardless. I didn't care; I had my set of friends, so I was good.

Nangie introduced me to her friend Vikki. Vikki and Nangie were around the same age; they were somewhat like best friends. Vikki was a light-skinned mixed girl with pretty hair. I enjoyed her company when we all walked home from school together. We became the three amigos.

We would hang out at each other's homes after school and on the weekends. Vikki's mom was kind of mean and strict, so we didn't go to her house that often. Nangie lived with her dad and sisters, and he was very laid back, so we spent most days at her house.

While hanging out with my two new friends, I met another girl. I thought she looked familiar from the school I attended when I was adopted. I discovered later on that we did attend that school together. She had been diagnosed with cancer at a very young age (actually right after Mrs. Robinson took me out of the school) and lost her leg. I began to hang out with her all the time too. She stayed a block away from my foster mother, so sometimes I would walk her home while pushing her in her wheelchair.

I started hanging out over her house all the time. I liked her mom. She was very friendly and understanding of my situation. She had a younger daughter and two sons that lived in the home as well. I would eat and hang out with their family as if I were a family member myself. This was my home away from home. My friend's mom decided to adopt me as her goddaughter since I'd never had one. She treated me like a biological daughter.

I began to get my itch for attention again. I was being picked on by all the females at school, so I figured I needed that male reassurance again. I got it. I would let boys feel on me passing them in the staircases and walking past them in the hallways. I always giggled; I thought I was that deal and that my body was too.

My older brother was attending school with me at this time. He caught me one day giggling at a boy who had grabbed a big handful of my butt cheek. He flipped out on me in front of everyone standing in the hallway waiting for the bus (dang near the whole school). He called me ho, slut, nasty—anything you could think of that would degrade and hurt a person's feelings.

Now I didn't mention this in the beginning of the story, but my brother and I did not get along to well. We were always arguing and fighting. I was angry with him because I got teased at all our schools because people thought he was gay. There was one point in time when we resided with the Robinsons that we got into a fistfight that had to be broken up.

Yeah, we weren't the best of buddies. So anyways, I began to immediately dog him out in front of everyone. I yelled in front of everyone about how he used to cry in his bed every night like a little girl, that he was gay and soft—anything I could say to get all eyes off me because of what he did.

I went home that afternoon with Nangie and Vikki. I met some light-skinned boy along the way, and we exchanged numbers. My guy friend would come over a couple of days out the week and sit with me. He was my boyfriend for a little while until he took my virginity without my permission.

We would just watch television and hang out like what teens do when they're bored. One day I decided to go to his house. I was sick of always being in my house. I was to be home by eleven o'clock, which was my curfew. I thought I was going to be just hanging out and watching movies, like we did at my house. I was in for a rude awakening.

We watched TV for a while and then he asked for me to come into his room. I was naive and assumed he had a gift or something hidden for me in his room. What I got was a surprise of my life that I was not happy about and did not want.

He pushed me down on the bed and began to kiss all over me. I told him I didn't want to have sex. I wanted to be a virgin till I got married. That's what I had been taught by Mrs. Robinson. He continued to touch and feel on me, steadily holding himself and trying to push my shorts and panties over.

I continued to yell no while pushing him in his chest and stomach, trying to get him lifted off me. Before I knew it, he had thrust himself inside me. The pain was excruciating. I gave up pushing and hitting him; he had made it in. It was pointless to fight any longer. I just laid there with tears strolling down my eyes. I told him I needed to be taken home; I was over my curfew.

He called a cab and took me home. He said he loved me, kissed me, and I got out the cab. Ms. Viriam was furious I had broken curfew, and she cursed me out. I didn't tell her what happened because she was already mad at me. She'd probably just said I was lying.

She knew my past history with the last foster mom. In a way, I felt it was my fault anyways. I shouldn't have gone to a boy's house that late, and I should have gone with a friend. I kind of felt it wasn't too big a deal because he was my boyfriend. So I moved on and let it go.

The next morning, I was bleeding and sore when I went to the restroom. I had no idea you bleed after losing your virginity, so I was confused and scared. I told Ms. Viriam what was going on. She thought I was just starting my period.

I thought someone broke into my room while I was sleeping and stuck a broom or something inside my vagina. It sounds stupid, but I honestly didn't know what the blood was. I had started my period two years ago, so I knew that wasn't the case. I broke up with him soon after that incident.

CHAPTER 10

I continued to run the streets with my friends, breaking curfews and being placed on punishment. After about six or so months, I asked my foster mom if she would take in my brothers and sisters in Kalamazoo. She thought about it for a while and decided she would. So after convincing my worker we needed to be together, it was decided they would come there with me. I was so excited to see them and was happy that they were living with me. They were excited and kind of sad because they had grown used to Ms. Karen and were torn between us two.

Christmas came, and we all were together. We received our gifts from our foster mom and some from the casa. I really liked the gifts from the casa; I didn't like the gifts from Ms. V. I was ungrateful and felt like I should have had more gifts. I sulked and complained the whole day. I ended up being sent to my room early.

Months went by, and I began acting the same way I did in the last foster home. This foster mom didn't give up quite as fast she sent me to a respite home. A respite home is a foster home that takes in kids when their original foster parents need a quick break. That's what she decided to do, thinking maybe I'd change my ways.

The respite foster mom was mean. She had a very stank attitude and wanted me to do everything around the house. Her own three children were treated like gold. I had to stay with her for two weeks. The only good thing about her house is that she cooked exceptionally well.

She had another foster girl there a couple of years younger than me. We spent most afternoons outside playing together and walking around. When my two weeks were up, I went back home. When I got back to Ms. V's home, I was told I was being removed from her home.

Once again, my things were packed up, and my worker picked me up and took me back to the group home. I was told I'd probably be here a little longer this time around. It wasn't going to be easy finding a placement with me being kicked out of two already. My brother was there as well. I was fine with staying at Kids First again. I liked that place. The staff was nice and so were most of the kids. So it was not an eye-opener for me; it was a delight.

I settled in once again and had another roommate this time around. She was a big girl—not too pretty but very nice. She was a promiscuous girl who talked about her sexual experiences all the time. My time was spent in my room reading and going down to the basketball court playing with the other residents.

There was a rec room in the basement where we had a pool table and different activities to keep us busy. I hung out down there a lot. There were a lot of kids that came in and out during my stay. I kept the same roommate until I departed.

The judge and the workers decided that it would be best if I was put in a long-term residential group home. They thought that would tame my inappropriate behaviors. I was shipped back down to Kalamazoo to do time in a full lock-down, long-term group home. I was to go to school on campus, and when I earned my levels, I could go off campus to school. I was a bad girl I guess.

The building was set way back in the middle of nowhere. There was nothing but open fields and trees everywhere. I guess this was to ensure no one ran away. If they did, they would get lost for sure and have no choice but to turn back. I was placed in the analyzing building first. This was a building where they watched your behaviors to see which specialized home to put you in. This home had about seven different sections to it. There were different boy homes for boys with different behavioral issues and about the same amount of homes for girls.

This temporary placement was strict. I could not have half of my belongings in my room. You had to earn your things back after they were taken to keep them in your room. The building was an all-white–painted brick inside. It was very basic. Tile floors were everywhere, even the bedrooms.

Our beds were buckled down to the floors, and the windows had wire grid covering them. It looked like what I thought a juvenile might look like. The staff was not as friendly as Kids First staff, so I could tell this was not a joke. My game was over!

I stayed in that building for about a month or more until they decided they would move me to the B-1 unit. That was a unit with the juvenile girls. Most of them had been arrested at some point of time, were violent, or kept running away from their biological or state-assigned homes.

As soon as I stepped into the new building, I was directed to a little room with a steel door. The door had a small opening at the top of it like a peephole. I was made to go inside that room and take my clothes off so the staff could ensure there was nothing on me. I might as well been in jail. That was so awkward!

After searching me, I put my clothes back on and was led down a long narrow hallway to my room. All the rooms had thick wooden doors with big silver automated locks on them. The small windows on the doors had grid on them as well as the one window in the room. There were no such things as having room-mates here.

Everyone had too bad of a past to be put in a room with another individual. Once again, all my things, CDs, radio, and my romance books were all taken. I wasn't allowed to have my rated-R CDs back until I left the program. I had to earn levels to have my radio in my room.

After my things were taken and the rest were put up, I was given a tour of the dungeon. There was the main living area. There weren't any couches; there were just big, hard plastic, cushioned chairs. Every chair that was used by one of the girls had their name on it. We had assigned seats!

Just off the main area was a large office area for the staff to write up paperwork or discuss things about us. The window on the office was very large; they wanted to make sure they could see everything. They had a control box inside that could lock all the doors automatically with one push.

Past the room I had been made to strip in was a bathroom. The bathroom was a big, tiled, white-walled room. It was a stand-up shower with different containers holding our soap, conditioner, and shampoo. We were not allowed to use our own products we'd brought in with us. We could earn those types of hygiene products out of a makeshift store they had there.

There was another bathroom on the opposite side set up the same way. The dining room was huge with big long tables in it. The kitchen was just off to the front of the dining room. There were only a few things in the kitchen, like snacks for the household. There was no preparing of meals in the home except on weekends and holidays.

I arrived around dinnertime, so everyone was gathered together and led out the house. Our food was prepared by staff members in a separate building where I'd also be going to school. The building was right down the sidewalk from our living quarters; it took less than two minutes to get there. When we arrived, there were already different groups of people in the dining hall—boys and girls.

There were about four separate areas with several tables in them. We set in the area right beyond the entrance. After some time, our house number was called. We all stood up and went up to the serving window in a single-file line. We were given a separated plastic serving plate, and each area was filled with food.

They made sure they covered all food groups. We ate our meal and went back to the building. We could either stay in the main area, watch TV, read, or hang out. I chose to go to my room and read a book. I did not like this place at all!

I was told by the other girls that there were sex offenders across the way, violent offenders down the way from them, and boys with more behavioral issues related to mental illness were just next to them. This place had people from all walks of life grouped together.

The next day, I met with the social worker that counseled our house. She discussed all the rules and procedures of this facility. The issues that had got me placed there were discussed and so were my goals that would get me out.

Now, in order to get out of this facility, there were different levels you must meet. Level 1 was the basics: keep your room clean, follow rules, and go to class. Level 2 was to meet your goals set up by the social worker. You only got a few short-term goals: follow rules and go to class. Level 3 is to complete all steps and long-term goals. Now the length of each level was spread out for a certain amount of time. It couldn't be made too simple or you'd get in and get right back out. They had to ensure that you were there long enough to learn your lesson.

My goals were an attitude adjustment—being respectful, obeying orders, and the basics. Once I made it to level 1, I could get my radio back and listen to music in my room. I could also earn a certain amount of points to buy things out the makeshift store. When I hit level 2, I could go to off-grounds school. So I had to be without music for a while and go to school in a big building right in the middle of the facility.

The school performed an education level assessment to ensure I got placed in the right classes. The classes were only half credits when transferring out to a regular school. I placed at the regular levels of someone in my age category, but my math was below average.

My English, however, was at a college sophomore level. I felt good about that one. (I smile as I write that part.) The classes were very basic and boring. I felt like they were not advanced enough for me. I got As on everything because my mind level was beyond the materials being taught.

CHAPTER 11

That group home was chaotic. There were always people fighting or attempting to run away. I can't say that I blame them; we weren't allowed to go anywhere or do anything. We sat in our units and in the school all day every day. Every now and then, there would be events on the campus where all units could participate in activities together.

I learned how to swim while I was there. They had a small dirty lake in the back of the campus where swimming in it was part of the evening activities. This was an activity where the two genders had to be separated, especially with the kinds of issues some of the boys had.

I earned my first level and was able to get my things in my room. I made my second level soon after. I was able to go off grounds to a regular school. I was picked up in the mornings by the school bus and dropped off afterward.

I enjoyed this school quite a bit. I experienced a few mean girls at this school but not as often like my previous high school. I had made a lot of friends, but once again, they were considered the outsiders. Once again, I didn't care. I had a group to which I belonged and could be myself.

Time went by and the home became worse. We got a few new girls in our unit that was pure troublemakers. We were always on automatic lockdowns; we'd be sent to our rooms and hear the clicks of the doors being locked.

I earned enough points to work in the campus kitchen. I was the person who put all the dishes in the dishwasher. I liked being able to get out the house and being active. That's when I discovered that some horrible things were going on.

There was a rumor going around that one of the nasty girls from the unit next to mine was sleeping with a male staff member. I told another staff member, and it was investigated. The other girls that had a crush on the same staff were pissed at me. They began to start things and talk about me. I felt so overwhelmed and stressed. I had my first anxiety attack ever and was rushed to the hospital.

By this time, I was already calling my lawyer and casa every day begging for them to get me out of there. They told me they were working on it. My casa worker came and visited me frequently. They allowed her to take me home and spend my Christmas vacation with her family for the entire second Christmas week of vacation. I discussed my concerns and fears with her and told her to stay working on getting me out. There were too many other acts of craziness during my stay there, and I was terrified.

There was a girl in our unit that I grew very attached to. She had my back through everything. The first fight I got into, she ran out her room and fought the same girl after me. She was my ace boon koon, aka my close friend. She and I were two peas in a pod; we did everything together. She was a chunky short girl with plenty of attitude and anger. I loved her. She was the realest girl I'd met in the home at the time.

There was an incident in the home where one of the residents tried to kill herself with a shoestring. Another girl I could not stand said that I was the cause of her suicide attempt. I thought that was the worst accusation ever. I leaped up to attack her.

I was instantly taken down by an overweight staff member who restrained me and tried to calm me down. I calmed down and was sent to my room where I punched the wiring over my window. I hurt my knuckles and bruised them, but I didn't care that was the closest I was going to get to relieve my anger.

CHAPTER 12

I had a lot of issues at that time. I was missing my mom more and more with each passing day. The things I was dealing with needed a mother's advice and love. I continued to cry and wonder about her every night. Was she thinking about me? Was she looking for me? Would I ever see her again? I began to write my emotions and feelings in a journal. That helped to release a lot of stress I was going through. Here are some inserts from my thoughts while living there.

December 25th, 2002

Merry Christmas Sophia! Today was the best Christmas ever. Oh my goodness I got so many presents from my casa worker and her family. I'm so thankful. They are the sweetest people I have ever met. I am so content. The Lord is so good to me. For the first time ever I had the best Christmas in my life.

December 26th, 2002

Today was a pretty boring day. We just sat in the house all day. I finally saw Lilo and Stitch. Actually I forgot we went to the movies to see Lord of the Rings Twin Towers, it was good.

December 27th, 2002

This is the day before I leave. So to make me happy on my last day I went skating with my casa's granddaughters. We got to head out by ourselves. Then we went to the movies to see Harry Potter by ourselves too. Then we went out to eat at Applebee's later on that evening. It was a pretty fun and full day.

December 28th, 2002

Today I go back to hell! Lucky me huh? My casa is taking me out to eat at one of my favorite restaurants. I left at 4:15 pm with my designated driver from hell and it was so packed in the van, it was horrible. I didn't get back to Lakeside to about 7:30. I rode in the van for about three hours than I came back to the cottage. Everybody acts like their excited about seeing me. Then I find out everybody's been talking about me. Why? I didn't know, but they just hating.

December 29th, 2002

Today was a pretty exotic day. Everybody was arguing about who was talking about me. I don't care no more!! I went to the mall and bought a shirt, a pair of pants, and two pair of shoes and some hairspray for my braids. Later on I was real dizzy so when I came back I went to bed. I slept from about 5:00 to 10:00 pm. Then I got up and ate and finished the book "A Child Called It" sequel, "The Lost Boy". Ta-Ta for now.

December 30th, 2002

Today one of the loco girls at Lakeside put her hand through a glass window. It was a real hectic day, it was too much drama for me. But I gotta go now. Bye-Bye. ~Phia~

December 31st, 2002

Today was a pretty good day. No good news and no bad news fa ya. So ta-ta for now. Write ya tomorrow.

CHAPTER 13

January 1st, "03"

Boring day ever even though it's New Year's it's just a regular day. When you locked up in placement, boring!

January 2nd

I had a good day until this evening I went loco. I'm tired of being at Lakeside and I want to know my real mom and my real siblings. I'm so lonely I feel like no one loves me! I'm depressed and scared. I don't know how long I'm going to be here now. How long is it going to take to find my real family? I'm just so depressed. God please help me!

January 3rd

One of the b—es that ran away is back again. Yessica already being two faced. Ain't that a damn shame! I asked for the pie Yessica's fat black a— threw the damn pie at me and the knife slid across the table and hit me. Today I was really mad for the first time since I been at Lakeside. When I get mad my cheeks jump my lip started jumping. I could've fought Yessica that's how mad I was I swear to you.

 Only person I feel like I can really believe, love, and trust is Roshanta. Sometimes I don't even know if I can trust her. It's so messed up. I'm slipping and don't even want to be a part of this world anymore now that's f—ed up! I'm supposed to be leaving real soon. I'm not getting my hopes up no more. So many people have told me so many things and promised me so many things and I've been let down!

 I don't know who to trust anymore. F— everybody. I don't care about anybody. I'm staying to myself till I get out of here! I'm cracking under pressure but I'm not gone break. I'm going to pray till I get up outta here. I'm gone keep faith. I'm leaving this month or the next. Please God don't let them keep me here any longer please Lord!

January 3rd

Today was a weird day. Yessica was back to her normal self. Sometimes I just don't understand her. I don't know what to do anymore. She is not right. I decided to just be her friend. I think she got good intentions but she just gets frustrated from being here. I'm frustrated from being here. Oh I forgot Danisha's back! I'm happy, I missed her a lot. My lawyer came up Friday. She told me I should be leaving soon. I pray to God their not lying to me again. Please get me outta here God!

January 6th

I forgot to tell you Danishas got a phone. I tried to call my ex yesterday, but I got no answer. Today I called this girl named Whitley she was real surprised to hear from me. But anyways Danisha got caught and they took her cell phone. She was pissed like a muthaf—a. She went to her room and packed her bags.

 Then she cussed the staff out and said they needed to call the police cuz she was gon act out. Then she started crying out of frustration and a few girls calmed her down. Then she started acting good. At a rate of ten I'd give this day a nine it was a little loco but overall good. Bye-Bye Journie.

January 7th, 2003

Nothing to say today.

January 8th, 2003

Today was a pretty sad day. Roshanta told about the plan that Danisha and Yess was planning to have Sose provoke Yamanda so she could lose her weeks. I agreed with them that she didn't deserve her weeks so I didn't make it no better. So I felt bad about indulging myself in peer negativity. Schipper, my social worker, finally showed me that she had some trust in me. She said she could see me leaving next month. I'm so happy now I really feel like I might leave. Please help me get out of here Lord! Amen!

January 9th, 2003

Today everybody got no access because we left the cafeteria dirty. I cried a lot today. I'm just really stressed. I'm ready to go. They also took everybody's cd's with inappropriate music on it. They always coming up with something new or old that hasn't been enforced. I can't take no more! I'm so f—ing sick of this place. It's breaking me down. But February is close! Praise the Lord! Hallelujah!

January 10th, 2003

Today I got into it with one of the staff members Rita. I don't know what to do anymore. She has favorites and I'm tired of it.

January 11th, 2003

I had a talk with Rita. She still is favortisiming. I was so good today. I hope I get good scores.

January 12th, 2003

What is her problem? All day she's been talking about everybody to that alien b— Chellele. Now I know was good and I wasn't talking about nobody. Rita still marked me down and I was good. I'm scared. I'm scared I'm not going to leave. Rita is going to hold me back by being mean. Every time I do be real good I still get marked down.

What am I supposed to do. I want to leave so bad. She can't hold me back. I can do it! I'm not gon let her bring me down because I know that's all she trying to do. But the thing that bothers me the most is that she talks about us to Challele. Challele is a child. Shouldn't nobody be discussed to a child.

Please help me Lord. Let me leave in February as planned I can't take it no more. Please help me God! Amen! I love you Lord. I might not show it all the time by my actions but I do. I think about you all the time it's just going to take time for me to trust anyone anymore. I'm sorry I've failed you Lord. Please forgive me. For now on from today I put my hand on The Holy Bible that from January 13, 2003 to the end of my life I will try to please you any way I can. When I make a mistake this time I won't give up on you or myself amen!

January 13th, 2003

Well Danisha befriended Challele again even though she talked about her the whole week. But oh well! Well that's all I really have to say! Oh yeah I finally told somebody that cared and believed me about Rita. She said she would take it to one of the staff meetings.

January 15th, 2003

Today was an okay day. Danisha is a b— and she fake all the way. One moment she talking bout a n—, next minute she in they face. I want to bash her boat head even flatter. She already got bags up under her eyes. I'll turn those black if she don't quit messing with my emotions and feelings like I'm a toy to use and throw away.

January 16th, 2003

Today was a very exotic and violent day. Danisha pushed me to the limits of wanting to fight her. I went to my room instead and fought the wall. I was so pissed I could've just strangled her or something. But I'm smarter than that. Scores: 100, 100, 88, imagine that!

January 17th, 2003

A very good day. I got a new schedule. I got swimming, drama, United States History II, and English. Day rating, 1-10 about a 9 or 10, very good day for me.

January 18th, 2003

Nisha back in my face again. I don't understand this dumb cottage. I'm doing the best I can cuz I don't know who to like, who to believe, or what to do period!

January 19th, 2003

I don't know why when I looked at my goal scores from last night they were lower. Especially my bottom goal. I bet you they did that just because I was talking to Danisha again cuz when we wasn't talking I got good scores. They probably think we talking about people just cuz she known for negativity. Just cuz she is and I'm talking to her don't necessarily mean I'm talking bout somebody. Oh well!

January 20th, 2003

Yes been acting like a bia, didn't really care for like the first time. I finally went back to church again. Praise you Lord for helping me out. I saw Ferria, Steve and the cute little baby. I also seen a couple of people who go to my school or that I've known in the past. Overall, a pretty good boring day.

January 21st, 2003

Nothing special today except my casa and my brother came to see me. We went to Fazzolis and the mall. They got everything on sale, name brand stuff for so cheap. I went to see the movie "National Security" that movie was off the hook and Martin Lawrence with his cute self, he crazy as heck. I love him. He seem so funny and nice. Overall day, 1-10, 10. Thank you Lord for letting me live another day.

January 21st, 2003

I'm so confused I don't know what to do. I'm going crazy. One moment I feel violent, next minute sad, happy, sad, and violent. I don't know maybe it's just pms. I'm so mad. Oh my God you just don't know how down I feel. I feel ugly and I'm scared to go swimming in front of everybody at school tomorrow.

Lord please help me be confident and strong. Help me not to care what anybody say about me. Lord help me to just try my best no matter what. Lord I'm giving up on having friends and even associates. Lord all I do to me is cause myself pain talking and playing with these girls. Lord please help me tomorrow.

I'm so scared to show my body. I feel like crying so bad but I'm holding it in. I don't even know if I got everything I need for swimming class. Day rate 1-10. I rate this day a 2. I'm pissed at the world and everything in it. Help me Lord, please help me Lord. I need you so much right now. Please Lord help me!

January 24th, 2003

I've been going through a lot for the past few days. I've had a very bad week. People been f—ing with me. I'm so sick of all these b— a— girls talking s—. Today Nangeo one of the boys on the campus, called me a b—. I said I'll show him a b—. Then this boy from Comstock named Oscar started f—ing with me.

He was trying to drag up old s— about what happened a long time ago. I still want to whoop this one b— a— (you know who it is). I hate

her so much. I used to love her so much. She
meant so much to me. She was like my sister.
Then I found out she was just using me. I'm so
hurt and confused. I don't know what to do no
more.

I can't give up I have to stay strong and keep
going. One of the girls here named Namanda
(the most true person I ever met). I loved her
so much I might not have acted like it, but I
did. She got discharged. I'm gonna miss her so
much. She was basically the only person I could
trust even though I got into a lot of fights and
arguments.

I still needed her. I'm gonna miss her so much.
Lord help me through this program cuz I need
her so much to talk to me. She gives me the best
advice I can get. Lord help me. Keep Namanda
safe and in good space. Ta-ta for now. Peace out
dawg.

January 27th, 2003

Sorry fa not writing ya but I been busy and for-
getful. I forgot to tell you I had court Monday.
Almost everybody wants me out of Lakeside
except for Schipper and Kelly. Danisha and
I were talking again. It ain't gon last I bet. It
never last more than two or three weeks. Oh
well. I gotta crush on somebody. He cute. Plus
I have some dudes I don't know grinning at me.

I must look good, huh! Well I G2G for now.
Bye. Peace out!

CHAPTER 14

February 8th, 2003

I'm sorry for not writing you in a long time.
I've been going through a lot for the past couple of weeks and haven't felt like writing lately.
But I'm going to tell you what's been going on.
I've been real stressed lately. I feel like I'm going
to die or have a nervous breakdown. I've been
calling my lawyers and my casa worker telling
them to please get me out of here because I
can't take it no more.

You practically have to be perfect to get out
this damn place! I hate this place so bad till it's
not even funny. I wouldn't recommend an ant
to live in this gotdamn pace. This place makes
people go crazy. More bad s— happens to people than good s—. Yesterday I had an incident
with this fat a— b— named Vikky, piggy a staff.

I was on nap because of something that had happened the day before. I glanced at the t.v. She hollers out "Sophia! No watching t.v., your first prompt" Okay fat a— b— is what I said. I turned to look at somebody. The t.v. is in the middle of the room. If I'm turning to look at somebody of course I'm going to glance at the t.v. when it's right in front of my chair. Dumb—! Fat a—, piggy a—, b— a— Vicky.

Gon say or should I say holler at me like she my damn mama and talking bout Sophia I just told you about watching t.v. I said dang Vikky, what's wrong with you. Fat a— got out her seat like she was about to do something. Talkin bout, you still looked at the t.v. even if it was just a glance. Big muthaf—in deal, s—! I said oh wow fat a—. I glanced at the damn t.v. big deal. Fat a— pig says, you're not taking responsibility.

 How?! You said I'm watching TV I just glanced at TV, two different things. "You're still not accepting responsibility. I guess I'm not than. Todays goal scores- 58, 75, 58. What type of bulls— is that? That fat a— b— gon mark down all my muthaf—in scores over that one gotdamn problem.

That's why I hate this gotdamn place cuz of dumb s— like that. That fat pig lookin b— did not have to mark up my gotdamn scores like that. I had been trying so hard to be good for these stupid b—es up here. You can't do noth-ing to please these gotdamn people in this b—. I hate that fat a— b—, she can kiss my muthaf—in ass for all the f— I care cuz I know I was good. So f— her fat piggy a—!

I guess had an attitude that day. I sound extremely angry. I was cracking up as I wrote this part because I had never been a curser, I could just imagine how corny I sounded while cursing like a sailor.

February 18th, 2003

I looked so cute today. I had on a blue shirt with a blue viser and some blue earrings. I thought I was the s—. I looked so pretty! I was so proud of myself. I looked so cute. I cried in school today, I know, but I don't want to get all the way into that discussion. Sorry for avoiding you again. I've been going through some s— lately. Sorry!

February 20th, 2003

It's these two b—es in my class. All they do is talk about people or should I say me. I don't even know them, but they just be yappin off at the mouth about me. I can't stand stupid hoes like them. They just feel like they gotta talk about people if they don't dress or act like them. But, oh well, like people tell me, dust them haters off!

February 28th, 2003

I hope Schipper got my discharge date. I was like Schipper, I have to talk to you. She was like I have to talk to you too. I was like you have to? Or want to? She said she had to and I would be happy. My casa worker called me and asked did I call her. I told her no, because I knew she was out of town. So I said it must have been my brother and she was like no the call was from Lakeside. That has me all anxious now. Something's going on! Bye!

I was discharged sometime after that last entry. Now there was a point in there where I was watching a Lifetime movie. In this movie, a little boy had been taken from his biological mom as well. Some years later he was reconnected. I cried my eyes out. I wanted the same. I was banned from watching Lifetime the rest of my stay. Now on to the next part of this story.

CHAPTER 15

I was moved back to Grand Rapids again. I was put into the long-term residential homes by Kids First. I was to live in Saint John's Home for six months. I had to go to school on campus here as well until I earned my levels to go to off-campus school again. The difference was this home was way more laid back.

We ate at the home; we were even allowed to eat and cook in our home. I had a room with a roommate. Nothing was bolted down so we could set our room up the way we liked. I began to writing again for a short time after getting there. Here are a few more diary entries for this placement.

March 27th, 2003

I came to Saint Johns. One of the rules is you can't watch TV. on weekdays. You start off on orientation and you only get to make one phone call a week for about 3-4 weeks. That's some flat out bulls—! I was pissed! This s— worse than Lakeside. Imagine me saying something like that. I don't think I'm going to do real good in this program. They might not have a lot of rules, but the ones they do have is to strict.

March 28th, 2003

This is my second day at Saint Johns. I had to go to the common room. I didn't get to go to school. I was very bored. I did nothing but sit there for the whole day. I took a nap and watched t.v. for about three hours and that was my agenda for today. Boring!

March 29th, 2003

I'm not going to survive in this damn place. I din already got into it with this b— named Liza. One of the staff brought me some jam for my hair. She gon get mad and start hollering at us, me and the staff (like I was supposed to know that I couldn't get hair grease). So I walked to my room and was like I'm not going to survive this place.

Than I came back out my room. She was still out there trippin. Than she was like she didn't have to get smart or make that smart comment when she went to her room. She was referring to me because I made a comment under my breath. I was like I wasn't getting smart. She rolled her eyes and was like, I wasn't talking to you.

I just walked away. I asked to get my stuff out the van and went to my room and slammed the door. P.S. Later on she apologized for being a b—. Oh yeah, we also went go kart racing at Craigs Cruisers. I crashed and bit my tongue so hard that it bled and it bruised. I f—ed up my thigh too!

I can barely bend it and my tongue hurts like hell and my leg. I ain't ever crashed that hard in my life. Imagine crashing in a real car. Oh my God that would be horrible wouldn't it? Well peace out. My arms tired.

March 30th, 2003

Today I just sat around watching Lifetime. It was kinda boring. Of course nothings completely boring if lifetime is involved with your day. But that's all I have to say about that.

March 31st, 2003

Tomorrow I start the fake a— school at Lakeside. Oops my bad not Lakeside, Saint John's Home. I kinda actually like this place. I can't wait till I get off orientation cuz than I can make 10 phone calls a week-beats Lakeside phone call times.

April 1st, 2003

I couldn't come up with no good April fools jokes. I wrote to three of my friends today. I wrote to Brittney and Felicia and Tricey. I was so excited to tell them about Saint Johns. I hope they write back. I don't think they will. But if they don't their not real friends anyway and I'm better off without them!

April 24th, 2003

I've been going through a lot this month. Boys, boyfriends, guys, talking nasty to me. I said I wouldn't respond but I've found myself breaking my promise to myself. I started going out with B-Dub....but it only lasted for three days. I found out he was messing with another girl. She and him both said it wasn't true.

I say f— them and they stories. They miss me though and I don't know if im going to back to being their friends or not. I miss B-Dub a lot though. I've always liked him when we started talking again; somebody came and f—ed it all up. (I had knew him previously from my freshman year in high school) I don't understand why boys ask you out and then don't want to claim you.

I be hurt by it but I try to hold it in acting like I don't care, but I just be fronting. I haven't found anybody I can really trust and love yet. That's ashamed. I'm supposed to be going out with a different boy now named Rickson. I don't know if I trust him, he goes to off ground school, he could be talking to anybody.

I'm so stupid. I don't know what to do. I don't ever remember to pray I guess I need to remember. But I be so depressed, I be giving up on God. P.S. My best friend, suppose-to-be boyfriend lives here and he's a bi***!

I was taken shopping at Meijer Department store. We had a group van that we all rode to the store in. Everyone was going back to school shopping. I was excited to get some new clothes. I needed some new clothes I couldn't fit any of my old clothes.

Those clothes were taken and given away to some of the smaller girls in the home. I went to the on ground schools and it was okay, the work was still too simple for me. I got all A's and B's in math. I was determined to earn my levels and get out of this special ed made school.

My birthday was coming up soon, my sweet 16. I was in Lakeside on the 15th birthday; I was missing my sweet 16th too. I was given money towards my birthday from Saint John's Home. I wasn't sure what I wanted to do yet. I was still a kid at heart because childhood was stolen from me. I missed and had loved my little Indian doll my adoptive mom had bought me years ago, so that's what I did.

I bought me a newborn baby doll, a bunch of doll clothes, and a bunk bed. I loved my sweet 16 presents I'd bought myself. It might have been young for my age, but it was something I always wanted and I got it. I was content!

Saint John's home was much better than Lakeside. I went to Michigan adventures for the first time ever. The whole house of girls that had the appropriate levels to leave off campus went. I had never been to a theme park before so I was extremely excited. The theme park was huge and I rode all the rides I could.

 It was a fun day. I had fun all the time at this placement. I was able to run around outside and enjoy life. It was much easier to make levels here. The staffs were so much friendlier and fair. We did activities all the time. Weekends were out days for the entire group of us.

 We all would pick what we wanted to do, bowling, movies, and pool whatever activity we could find to do outside the home. We went to a lot of Whitecaps Baseball games at the Fifth Third Ballpark. I have to say at my age, I still miss Saint Johns and sometimes wish I was young enough to live there again. It was a great atmosphere.

I found my first love there. He was a short, dark skinned, chunky guy. He was so sexy to me, I developed a crush on him the first day I saw him. We flirted with each other and began going out. It was like a jail love. We couldn't actually be together in a boyfriend-girlfriend manner, but we were boyfriend and girlfriend no matter what.

We would always hope that our homes would go to the basketball court at the same time so we could each other. We looked forward to seeing each other in the on ground school. He was my boo. I was happy and smiling whenever I saw him.

I gained about sixty pounds after just a couple of months of being there. There were no restrictions on our food limits. Our refrigerator was always full of snacks and goodies. I ate out of boredom. So within a couple of months I went from a size 5 to a size 14. I was huge and swollen looking. I felt good about it though, I always heard guys talking about how thick a chick was, so I just knew I looked good. I continued my on ground schooling and earned my level within a short period of time.

When I earned my level to go to off grounds school, I was put back in Ottawa Hills High School. I was pissed off. I hated this school and the people in it. The same people that were there before were still attending the school. Most of the people I remembered didn't remember me. I use to be a "skinny minny," now I was "chunky monkey." I was asked for weeks what happened to me. Where I had disappeared to and how I got so big. It was people talking to me that had never talked to me before. I just humored them and remained cordial.

CHAPTER 16

I was doing great at Saint Johns. I was passing through all my levels. I never caused any problems or was in trouble for anything. I had learned my lesson living in Lakeside; I didn't want to get sent back there, so I did my best to behave. I remained at Saint Johns for about six months and was discharged.

I went to live in a foster home with a mid-age husband and wife and their three kids. It was an okay home. They lived in an old white house on a busy street down from another corner store. It was a pretty laid-back home. There weren't too many rules, and I had my own room and my own TV; I was good. I continued to go to school and do what I had to do.

This new family was okay. The couple had three kids—two together, and the eldest was the woman's child from a previous relationship. Their eldest was a girl about three years younger than me and the other two were young boys in elementary school. My stay there was kind of iffy. My foster mom and I clashed a lot. She always had an attitude and a smart mouth and so did I, so we always got into altercations. She hated my attitude, but I was born with it. It wasn't going anywhere, so "whatever" was my mind-set.

During my stay there, I met my high school sweetheart. He was a grade above me; I was a junior at this time. Weston was a tall, light-skinned boy with long thick hair that he wore in braids. He was known for being very good at basketball. He had been on the homecoming court the year before, so he was pretty popular.

He was the type of guy I always wanted to be with. At the time that I met him, he was talking to someone else. This girl was way too young for him, and when I began to talk to him, he lost interest in her. That did not go over well with the girl.

She started so much drama over Weston. They weren't even dating at the time; they just talked to each other between classes and during lunchtime. This girl had all of her friends not liking me and talking about me every time I passed one of them in the hallways. All of them together would just giggle and whisper whenever they saw me. They were younger than me and were childish, so I just tried to ignore them.

Weston and I grew closer as time went by. We did everything together. I went to his house every day and would stay until it was time for me to go back home. I became a part of his family. The more time we spent together, the more comfortable we became with everything. That caused more issues at my foster home.

We were almost caught several times having sex in my bedroom. My foster dad was the one who always popped his head in on us. They'd be gone when I'd come home so we'd try to hurry and sneak some loving in. I didn't care, though, that's why I continued to do it. Half the time my foster parents were fighting and arguing, and they always took that on all of us kids. I did certain things out of spite because some things weren't fair or right.

I decided during my summer break that I wanted to get a job. When I was adopted, the parents changed my last name out but not the rest of my name. I requested to be given my original last name back when the adoption broke. When I was ready to work, I had to wait for my birth certificate to be redone and certified.

It was also coming all the way from Milwaukee, Wisconsin. When it finally arrived, I found me a part-time job at a McDonald's. It was an okay job for about two months. I was tired of waking up early for the breakfast shift, and the evening shift was too hot for me to walk there. It was about six blocks from my home. I quit the job before school started back.

My birthday and Christmas were horrible there! On my seventeenth birthday, my foster mom bought me a pair of sweatpants and a shirt. They were both cheap and plain. My birthday is in July. Why the hell would she buy me sweatpants? I was pissed.

To top it off, she bought a lemon cake. I hate lemon cake; she loves lemon cake. Who buys a cake for someone's birthday and not even ask them what flavor they like? A mean person who doesn't really care because you're not their kid anyway.

On Christmas morning, I opened up mainly clothing boxes. All the boxes had capris and pants in them. All of them I could not fit; they were two times too big for me, and I asked about the capris. She said it was for the summertime, they were on sale. When I asked why she bought everything too big for me, she stated that my weight moves up and down all the time. Bullcrap! I hadn't gained or lost weight in almost six months. With the amount she got for me every month, she could have done better for me on my birthday and Christmas.

My CASA worker came shortly after I had opened up my gifts. My casa worker had bought me everything. I had as many boxes under the tree as her grandchildren. She had bought me books, clothes, hair accessories, shoes, gift cards—everything I could think of or that would make me happy was under the tree.

I enjoyed a giant Christmas dinner with her and her entire family. When I came back to my foster home, my foster sister told me she had heard her mom talking on the phone. She said that her mom had told someone about my behavior behind opening up my gifts. Her mom told them that I was not her daughter anyway so she didn't really care that I was mad about the gifts. I knew that was the reason, so it didn't surprise me at all.

CHAPTER 17

During my year-long stay with this foster mom, I did exceptionally well in school. I averaged a 3.8 my junior year in high school and a 4.0 on my last semester. The following year, I was to take just two classes at the high school and two classes at the community college. I was so excited, and I felt so smart.

I was a college student at seventeen years old! I signed myself up for creative writing class and criminal justice. I loved writing, so I was very excited to see the college aspect of my favorite subject. Since I was only going to school half days, I decided to get another job. I was hired for a part-time position at Popeye's Chicken. I basically ran the cash register and packaged the food for the customers.

I took criminal justice because I always wanted to be a lawyer. I didn't do too well in that class. I was always under my boyfriend and hanging out at his house during that class. I did very well in my creative writing, however. There were a lot of poems I'd written for one of my assignments, and my instructor wanted to publish half of them.

I never went back for him to do that. I had gotten As during the entire semester, so I figured there was no point of going back for the finals. I got a B+ in that class. Pretty good for a first timer that didn't even do the final, huh?

I will always remember the prom of my high school sweetheart. I was to go with him as his date for the night. I told my foster mom. She didn't want to buy me a dress or anything. She went to their older friend and got me an oversized, old and aged cream bridesmaid's dress. She got me a dress that her thirty-something-year-old friend had worn to a wedding with some ugly-strap shoes.

I felt so ugly and stupid. I looked like an old woman. That was supposed to be a day where you feel beautiful like Cinderella after the fair godmother's visit. I felt like the "before" Cinderella. I looked horrible. To top it off, she had my hair done cheaply as well. The lady brushed my hair up with a bunch of gel, which made my hair poof, and put a fake ponytail on it. That was it.

When I went to the prom, all the girls looked like they stepped out of magazines. They had makeup on, fancy dresses, and beautiful hairstyles. I felt like an odd ball out. Of course everybody wanted to be nice to me. All the girls would say "Awwww, you look so pretty." I knew they were lying. I'd smile unsurely and say thank you. It was a bad and embarrassing night for me—a great disappointment for me.

After my year at this foster home, I figured I had all I was willing to take. I was tired of the constant fighting between me and my foster mom and her and her husband. I was ready to leave. Her husband was too sneaky and slick with his words and his doings.

He made me nervous. I didn't trust too many males, and he was one I got a bad vibe from. I decided I would go stay with my foster mom's sister who also had a foster license—biggest mistake I could've made.

They say the grass isn't always greener on the other side. They weren't kidding. The grass was brown and dying on this side. I would have been better off staying where I was. Her sister was the most vindictive, childish, and immature woman I'd ever met.

She loved drama. Living with her and her two teen daughters was like being in high school. They were like the kids at school that picked and taunted me all the time just to be mean. She had a preteen son as well, but he didn't indulge in the bullying that the others were doing.

During my three-month stay there, I engaged in more arguments with the girls and their mom than I had in school. The sad part is that their mom started majority of the catfights. She would pick on me as soon as I came through the door.

I was working and going to college at this time, and as soon as I would make it home, I was bombarded with someone in my face cussing me out or starting something. I was determined to go to college and work and ignore them, but they would not let me.

I didn't go to the prom on my senior year. I was so embarrassed about the year before. I didn't want to put any effort or time into the event. I decided to buy some white slacks and a red ruffled shirt and go to dinner with my high school sweetheart, Weston. We went to T.G.I. Fridays with my one of my girlfriends and had a nice rib dinner. We shared a drink, stories, and laughter.

I had fun that night. I didn't need to go to the prom with all the stuck-up cliques I attended school with. As long as I was with him, it didn't matter to me. I had enjoyed my night. I had a job this time around, so I paid for my own outfit. I had my wonderful god mom who paid her cousin to do my hair. For once, I looked good. I felt beautiful that night.

One of the younger girls jumped in my face one evening after coming home. She said she wanted to fight me and was cursing. When I began to curse back at her, her mom ran up the stairs and started yelling at me. I said right then and there that it was time for me to go.

I got my phone and my purse and left. That was the first time I ever ran away. It became too much for me to deal with, and I was not about to fight a thirteen-year-old girl with me being seventeen. That was completely inappropriate, and they just wanted to push me to that limit so I could end up in lockdown again. It wasn't about to happen.

While I was walking down the sidewalk, the foster mom sent her daughters after me to snatch my phone out my hand. They were trying to make sure I couldn't call anyone, but I had already called Weston. He was advised of the whole situation and was on his way to get me. About five minutes later, Weston's mom was calling him and cursing him out about me.

My foster mom had called her when her daughters brought my phone to her. She had told his mom that I was cheating on him. She said I was talking about him behind his back and that I treated him bad. His mom was hysterical, so we decided I needed to go elsewhere to stay the night until I could reach my worker in the morning.

I went and stayed with my god mom that night. The next day, I called my worker and explained the situation. She instructed the foster mom to give the phone to her and went and got my belongings from her house. I had the cell phone cut off on the woman anyway before she could start anymore drama.

I had to call the phone company and have it reactivated. After getting my things back, I looked through it all and realized that my large CD case was missing. I had over eighty CDs in there. When my worker questioned the woman's daughters about it, they claimed they had not taken them; there was nothing more that could be said or done. I never saw my CDs again.

I wanted to stay with my god mom until my eighteenth birthday because it was only about two months away. My worker said she'd look into it. She did, and they found out that my god mom had a police record, so my request to stay was denied. However, just because of all that had happened, she did allow me to stay for two weeks until the found a foster home for me.

They didn't find a foster home in the allotted time; so once again, I was forced to go back to Kids First. I already knew everything, so they just showed me where my room was, and I went on about my business. My worker found me a foster home about a week later.

They moved me back out of Kids First and took me to my new foster home. I was to stay there until my eighteenth birthday, and then I was getting my first apartment. I had been attending an independent living class the last four or six months before my eighteenth birthday.

By the time I moved in this home, I had quit Popeye's and began working at Meijer with Weston. I had a bunch of money saved up and brand-new furniture put up in storage, I was ready. I continued my classes and continued working so I was barely at home. My foster mom had a bunch of foster daughters and one boy—it was a full house. I enjoyed my time out because it was such a busy atmosphere.

I graduated from high school on May 26, 2005, with a 4.0 grade average. Weston, my god mom, and my CASA worker attended the graduation ceremony. After my graduation and mingling with other classmates, Weston and I went out to a restaurant for dinner. Since I had been moved around so many times during my senior year, I had no one to throw me an open house party.

The staff at Saint John's Home threw an open house housewarming party for me. Weston, his mom, my casa worker, and the staff at the group home were the only people that attended. It was a very plain, lonely open house. I felt like a reject, but I was thankful for those that did come.

Weston's mom had bought us so many things for the new apartment. I was extremely pleased and grateful. Weston's mom had always looked out for me since me and Weston began to date. She bought me gifts on every holiday and for my birthdays; I was treated like a daughter-in-law instead of a girlfriend. I call her an angel in disguise. My CASA worker also bought a bunch of things as she always did. It was a pretty good turnout overall; I just wish it could have been more people and been thrown by family and friends. I didn't have the average life, so I couldn't expect too much.

Five days after my eighteenth birthday, I was renting a U-Haul truck and moving into my new one-bedroom apartment. That was the most exciting day of my life! No more foster home and group home living for me. I was free—finally! I had a red sleeper sectional, a coffee table set, gold and white bedroom set, and a wrought-iron glass table with four chairs. My little apartment was so cute and stylish. I was ready to take on the world.

CHAPTER 18

I know a lot of people wonder what goes through a person head when they're no longer a ward of the state. People ask me if I was scared, did I feel abandoned, and what I was feeling. I felt a sense of relief. I was happy, prepared, and ready.

I didn't mind being dropped out of the system. The system caused me more pain and grief than anything. I wasn't scared because I knew I was a smart girl, and I was determined. I was too scared to fail and be without, so I knew I would try my hardest to survive in the world by myself. Not having family to fall back on and depend on if I was ever hurt and down was the main factor that kept me going. I knew I had no one there for me so I focused myself.

I decided to find my adoptive mom, Mrs. Robinson, after I graduated. My adoptive dad was older when I was adopted, so he was definitely old by this time. I wanted to be reunited with him and spend time before God decided to take him home. I found them shortly after looking around. I had seen my adoptive mom's daughter at a store and got their number.

I began spending time with both of them. One thing that I don't do is hold grudges against people. I had long ago forgiven my adoptive mom; my life could have been worse. You have to count your blessings through any situation, and I'd counted a few as I grew older.

My adoptive mom would invite me and Weston over for dinner, and sometimes she would come visit me at my home. One day, I decided to ask her the biggest question ever. "Why did you abuse us?" She told me that she never abused any of us, and it was all Fancy's doing. She said that we were heathen children and didn't know how to let her and her husband love us, especially me. I'm pretty sure I was old enough at the time to remember her abusing me.

Two months later, I was pregnant with a baby boy by Weston. He and I had begun to live together. I went back to school while pregnant and took a few courses. Halfway through my pregnancy, Weston lost his job. He had been at Meijer since he was sixteen years old; he was twenty-one when he messed up his job.

So I was working full time now. Pregnant and big, I was a greeter at Meijer. So for eight hours a day, I was on my feet, standing by a cold door in the winter and a burning hot door in the summer. I was tired and big and ready to have this baby. I was too young to be doing so much. I was pregnant at eighteen, working full time, and trying to go to school.

Toward the end of the pregnancy, I discovered that Weston had been talking to his ex behind my back. While I was at work big and tired, he was at home relaxing, doing nothing while telling his ex he loved her and wanted to be with her again. He had been texting her that he still loved her and wanted her back.

That broke my heart. I was carrying a man's firstborn son, and we were living together. Behind my back, he was telling another woman he loved her but was telling me he loved me too. We got into it real bad the night. I found those texts, but I forgave him that following day. I had my son on Mother's Day, May 9, 2006. He was named Ivaun Jay Ford. Ivaun was a large eight-pound baby who was twenty-one inches long. He looked just like his dad; they were spitting images of each other.

Weston and I started splitting up constantly right after the birth of our son. We were arguing and fighting all the time about any and everything. I was still harboring the fact that he had attempted to cheat on me. I could not let it go that easily. What if he did it again? So I'd put him out for a few days then would let him back into our home.

We never messed around sexually again after I found the texts. Six months after our son was born, I decided I wanted out the relationship. Weston was very in love with me and was not giving up that easily. From the time that I made my decision to the time that we split, Weston begged and pleaded for me not to end our two-and-a-half-year relationship, but I had my mind set.

I gave Weston all our apartment furniture and bought myself all new furniture. Weston didn't have any money saved, and he had just gotten a new job. He was going to get his own apartment, and he needed furniture, so I gave up all the furniture I bought. We both went our separate ways. I decided to move on the far end of town. Weston moved about four blocks away from where we had previously lived.

I had a two-bedroom, two-bathroom apartment, and Weston had a one-bedroom apartment. I maintained my apartment by myself very well. I was the only one who took care of the household when I was with my ex, so I had no problem being on my own. It felt good to live by myself; everything was so relaxed and calm every day. Weston would come get his son when I had to work, or I would drop our son off to him on my way to work.

Not too long after our breakup, I met a guy at my job that I really liked and began to mess with him sexually. He was much older and more experienced than me; I learned a lot from him. I was his sideline girl though. He had a girlfriend that he lived with, and they had a child together.

He would always say that he didn't want to be with her, that she was psycho and wouldn't let him go. I believed him and continued to mess with him anyways. He winded up going to jail. I decided to let it go then. His voice was no longer in my ear convincing me to believe his lies, so I was free-minded.

CHAPTER 19

I met my youngest son's dad about a month after the previous guy friend went to jail. I was hooked up with this guy that my now ex-friend had set me up with. She had told me about two different guys. I thought that I was meeting the first guy she had told me about.

The next day after meeting him, she told me that he was the guy she had told me about who was on parole and had just six years in prison for armed robbery. He was twenty-five years old when I met him. That means he was eighteen when he was locked up.

After I found out, I decided that I did not want to talk to him again. I had never messed with a convict before. The friend convinced me that he was a good guy and had just been young and dumb. Three weeks later, I was pregnant by him with my second child.

I moved a little too quickly and was irresponsible in not using protection. That's something that's obvious, and I have no problem admitting my stupidity. We were both upset about it and decided that I would get an abortion. I had my date set up for the abortion and was ready for it to be over with.

I knew it was too early to be having another kid. I was only nineteen years old and on my second pregnancy. My son was only ten months. The day before I was to get the abortion, the dad changed his mind. He looked like he was going to cry when I gave him the date and time. I was still determined to get rid of the baby. I changed my mind later on as well.

He ran the streets and messed with other women. I just continued to throw up and be sick every morning by myself. I was lonely, and I knew I was going to do this pregnancy alone. I wasn't ready for that, but I had no choice now.

I was too far along to get an abortion at the time when I realized I wasn't going to have any help. About two months later, my baby's dad decided he wanted to come and live with me so he could be there for the pregnancy and me, I thought. I had another thing coming.

This man was so angry inside. He treated me as if I owed him something just because majority of his adult life had been taken by the system. Every other day it was an argument and fight in our household. I had a very depressing pregnancy.

I cried and stressed every day. I was working, pregnant, and taking care of a one-year-old child while my man ran the streets in my car and did nothing. He was a drug dealer making money but never paid a bill. It was the worst experience I'd ever had with a man.

I was desperate and didn't think I could get any better than what I had, so I dealt with it. I dealt with his putdowns and negativity. I did not want to be pregnant alone, so my mind-set was, "Anything was better than nothing." Things were 80 percent bad and 20 percent good.

He had his good days where he'd stay in the house and watch movies to spend time with me. We would make banana splits—his favorite—and just relax. Out of the seven months we were together, he only took me out on one date and bought me one thing.

He continued to do what he wanted the entire relationship. When he wasn't yelling and making me feel bad, he was out all day and night in my car. When my car had mechanical problems, he never once contributed any money to get it fixed. I was the one who gave him his startup money to buy the drugs to distribute.

I never saw a dime more than what I let him borrow. He brought in hundreds a day, and whenever I asked for anything, I was yelled and cursed out. He was a mean, evil, bitter, and selfish man. I tried so long to make it work, thinking I could help him see that he had a good girl. I was willing to help him and do anything for him.

I gave birth to his firstborn son November 22, 2007, at around 12:03 a.m. Jamond Deont'e Seals was seven pounds, three ounces, and twenty inches long; and he was my Thanksgiving baby. He was a gorgeous little person, so bright and new. He looked just like his dad from head to toe. My baby's father and his family were in the delivery room when I had him, and everyone jumped up and down with joy after I pushed him out.

The next day, my son's father and his family came up to the hospital. No one had a Thanksgiving plate for me, not even a balloon or a gift in sight. My son's father came up there driving my car and with a new pair of hundred-dollar timberland boots, without a flower or card in hand. My feelings were so hurt; I carried a baby for nine months, went through twelve hours of labor, and didn't get anything—not even a thank-you or congratulations.

My son's dad came to get me and take me home the next day. Still, no flowers or balloons entered my hospital room. I got dressed and sat in the wheelchair while they rolled me out. I thought that maybe there would be something waiting for me at home, a surprise. We went home in pure silence in the car the entire way.

I climbed up the three flights of steps and opened up my door to nothing once again. I sat down with my newborn son and grabbed my eldest son so he could see his new brother. He took off running down the hallway. I don't know what he thought the baby was, but he was scared.

I received no kiss, no hug, no congratulations, or thank-you from my son's father. He told me that he was going to a bar with his stepfather and uncle later on that evening. He went into my dining room and sat down by the table and began to bag up his weed. Twenty minutes later, I decided it was time to say something.

When I asked him about his lack of attention and gratitude, he began to yell and curse at me. I asked him for something to eat, and he made me a dry bologna sandwich with no mayonnaise (which I hate, sandwiches without mayonnaise) and sat back down to bag his drugs.

He went out that night and came back around one or two the next morning. I was asleep, but he woke me and the baby up. After calming the baby down and feeding him, we both went back to sleep. The next few days were busy and hard with the new addition.

About a week later, my son's dad gave me a random card with no signature, which was not related to my giving birth, and a Christmas holiday–stuffed animal. He just said, "Here," and walked off with an attitude. I took the stuffed toy and threw it.

Christmas came around, and I made my first holiday dinner. It was my first time to make a ham. We sat down for dinner, and he complained that the ham was too tough. I put the ham back in the oven and called my eldest son's granny, asking for directions as to how to soften the ham. I took it out some time later, and he still complained that it was too tough for him to eat. I gave up trying to make it right, and I ate my ham and the other foods I had prepared.

He gave me one gift, which was a pair of Timberlands he had gotten on clearance at an off-brand (generic) shoe store. I did not mind the fact they were knockoffs, but I didn't like the style of the boot. I told him he could take the boots back and get the money so I could pay a bill. I had been off work since I had the baby, and he wasn't giving me any money.

He yelled and went on about how ungrateful I was, telling me to take the boots back myself and pay the bill. I asked him for his part of the bill money for the month. He stated that he had bought me a Christmas present, so why should he have to pay bills that month? I stated that I paid $595 in rent that month, so what about me?

I was told to use the money I would collect when I returned the boots back to pay the bills. That was not a fair deal. How could he tell me to take things back that he's bought for me? That was Indian giving. To tell me to take my present back to pay my bills when he owed me the bill money regardless? He left me the next day. I was called all types of names, and he just complained and disrespected me the entire time he packed his things. It was my first time ever to be called out of my name by a man. I was hurt and shocked. He never gave me his part of the money for the bills.

He decided to move in with his stepdad. A couple of weeks later, he called and apologized for his behavior. We made up and talked about the breakup. He would come get his son several days a week to spend time with him. I would go over there sometimes just to sit with him and the baby.

We would talk and hang out. We thought that maybe we could make it work from a distance. It lasted for about two weeks, and then he began to mess with other women again. So we parted ways. I was a single, twenty-one-year-old mother with two kids, dumped with a two-month-old baby.

CHAPTER 20

I went back to work and took care of myself and my children. I had to stay focused and keep moving forward even though I was down and alone. I climbed those three flights of steps with groceries and with one kid on my hip and one behind me. No one was going to do that for me but myself. I had gotten myself into this situation, and I had to deal with it by myself. No matter how hard it was going to be, I wasn't going to let the negative side of my situation defeat me.

I continued to deal with the bull crap from my son's dad. A few months later, I started seeing him driving around a Dodge Durango truck. I questioned him about it, and he stated that it was his car. I was furious. This man left me, paying only a few bills, after I took care of him for months, and now he goes and gets a car?

I called him repeatedly for hours, cursing him out and presenting him with every bad thing that he had ever done to me. He had left an old, big screen TV in my house when he moved out. He asked me for the big screen back, but I told him no. He owed me money; there was no way he was getting the TV back.

Several hours after our altercation, my son's father was outside my apartment with his mom and a group of guys. He had borrowed someone's pickup truck. He was going to try to scare me into giving him the TV. In the middle of my apartment complex parking lot, he stood and cursed me out. He told me to do some vulgar things, that he never loved me, and that he had cheated on me the entire pregnancy.

His mom who was around fifty-eight years old started calling me b— as well. She stated that I was just jealous that I had no mom and, aha, that I didn't have family, that my mom gave me away, and that I should tell that b— (my mom) to get off crack. I had never experienced such ignorance and disrespect from people that I had a blood connection with.

That was the last straw. I cut him and his family off from my son. I would not have that type of negativity around me or my boys. I received something in the mail about three months later stating I was to be in court for a custody hearing for my youngest son. My son's father had gotten a job.

Now it would be easier for him to fight for visitation on the weekends and several days throughout the week. I winded up passing by him before we went into the courtroom. He pleaded with me not to tell the judge about his drug dealing; he really loved and missed his son. I knew he had genuine love for his son, so I decided not to argue the case.

I wish I would have. He was awarded visitation for three days out of the week and every other weekend. He was to pick him up and drop him off per the court ruling. He lost his job about a week after he had won the case and would refuse to drop him off at the times he was supposed to. He would make me come and get him instead.

Every time I'd go get my son, he would call me b— and talk about me while he put him in my car. He was just mean and disrespectful because he knew there was nothing I could do now that he'd won visitation rights. He took full advantage of the situation, causing me pure hell.

I started to focus on myself only and decided to start looking for my biological family. I had been wanting to look for them for years but had to wait until I turned eighteen. When I turned eighteen, I winded up pregnant, going to school, and working, so I never had time. I had a long conversation with a girl I had worked with at the time.

I had told her my life story, and I had gotten a few details from my adoptive mom about the situation that caused my adoption. My adoptive mom had told me she didn't know the name of the agency but knew it started with the word *green*. I told the girl that, and she looked up agencies in Detroit, Michigan, with the name *green* in it. She found the agency a few minutes later. I called the next day.

The lady at the agency asked me a few questions so she could find my file and let me know if my biological mom had signed a release form. A release form is to give permission to the biological parents' children to look for them by getting all the information the agency last had on them. Luckily, my mom had signed the waiver, saying she wanted to be found if her kids ever came looking.

I sent a copy of my ID and was mailed a large manila envelope full of documents. It had the names and birth dates of all my siblings and my mom's siblings. On the form, I discovered another sibling's name on the paper. My mom had another daughter about five and a half years later.

I was so disappointed when I read the file. It was pretty crappy stuff in there about me. The foster mom I was first placed with was telling the workers I was sexualized. She claimed that I walked around in public touching myself. There supposedly was an incident of me *oooing* and *ahhing* at a foster cousin while she washed my vaginal area. Ms. Jonsas had claimed that all I talked about was sex, and she had to watch me at all times.

It was so sad to see those things. I always wondered why I carried butterflies in my stomach from such a young age. I was told by my worker that I was caught humping and touching other kids. My foster mom claimed I would follow men around in a grocery store, trying to get attention.

I hate the way they make me look in the report. It was a horrible picture painted of me. I looked like a sex-craved baby. At first, I didn't believe any of it until I read further on. They had me examined by a psychiatrist who stated that every time he talked about anything I talked about sex and food (this is what I read in the report sent to me).

They talked about how smart my brother was. How he was involved and alert. Then they would talk about how I tried, but I wasn't as smart as him. How he could sing and how I tried to be like him, so I got an A for effort. That package of papers sent to me about the beginning of my life killed my heart. If I wasn't that smart, it wasn't my fault. My mom obviously didn't take an interest in me. It's not that the reports were a hundred percent accurate; there is a high possibility that a lot of the stories could have been fabricated.

I doubt she took any time to teach me anything. I felt like an idiot looking at the things documented about me. I was embarrassed for myself. Like I said, my life has been hell and gruesome since the day I was born. I guess it's my fate.

It also talked about my mom's feelings toward me. In the report, the workers stated that my mom had no interest in me. She paid attention only to my big brother. They would have to remind her I was there. She also paid no attention to my little sister. They stated that she had told them I was a "dark baby."

She was caught pinching and yelling at me several times and saying I was her "demon child." Wow. A demon child, my mother called me, but I was the one who cried for her for years. That hurt my heart to the core. To know that the person you have been looking for never really liked you is a dreadful feeling. I cried on and off that whole day.

I took my information straight from the Internet. I had seen a website advertised on the Maury Show that was supposed to help people find information on lost loved ones. The website said it needed eighty-something dollars. That frickin' website took a $180 from me. I was pissed. The website had all my old info, and nothing was accurate at all. It had nothing I needed. It basically stole all my money and gave me no results.

I browsed around and found another site where I could obtain some information on my family for $2.99. I decided to take another chance. It worked, but the number it gave for my mom was already disconnected. I tried a number for one of my aunts that were listed on the paperwork, and it was disconnected as well.

I was just about ready to give up when I decided one more name. I tried one of my uncles. It worked! A man answered the phone, and I asked for the name on the paper. He told me he wasn't there. My heart dropped instantly.

I asked him if he would tell the man that I was the daughter of his sister and gave him her name. He told me he was my uncle as well. He gave me his name, and sure enough, he was listed on the paper as one of my uncles. I now have three altogether and two aunts. We talked on the phone for a good thirty minutes. He told me he wasn't sure where my mom was.

She was a flighty person who moved a lot and changed her number often. He said he would try the last number he had for her, though. He called the entire family within ten minutes. Calls came streaming through, but not one was from my mom. It was an exciting moment for me, a moment that I had been anticipating my entire life.

My aunt who lived in Alabama was extremely excited; she just talked away for about an hour or two. She let me talk to my little sister (the last daughter my mom had) whom she had taken into her home for my mom. We both talked for about twenty minutes. My aunt then proceeded to call my other aunt as well on three-way. Everyone talked on the phone for about two hours. I called off from work and spent the day reuniting with everyone over the phone.

I had both aunts in Alabama, one uncle in Kalamazoo, Michigan, and two uncles still in Detroit, Michigan. They were scattered everywhere. I was kind of disappointed because that meant I could not see my aunts and sister like I wanted. My aunt wanted to see pictures of me, but I had no Facebook page or anything so she could see me and my kids.

I rushed over to one of my foster mom's house so that my foster sister could take pictures of me and my kids. We posted them up on Facebook immediately and I called my aunt and let her know. She was so excited, saying I was absolutely beautiful and so were my boys. She and I talked all day.

While I was preparing to go to bed after washing dishes and cleaning up my kitchen, my mom called! This was the most exciting call I've ever had in my life. I just listened to her voice and stood still, stuck. This was my mommy. The woman I had wondered and cried over for years. I had finally found her seventeen years later.

It felt so good to hear her voice again. We talked for around twenty minutes, then she said she had to go because she was a hustler, and she was trying to detail someone's car. That upset me, but I let her go. All these years missed and cleaning someone's car was more important than catching up with me; it was disappointing.

She didn't call for a few days actually. That hurt my feelings. I couldn't get a hold of her either those days, her phone was cut off. When she did call, she told me she was living in a woman's home and was basically homeless.

She asked if she could come stay with me. I didn't even know her. I had just found her, and she already wanted something from me? I told her I had to think about it; I didn't know if it was something I was willing to do that quickly. She said okay and didn't call me for a week.

I talked to everyone about the question she had proposed to me. I talked to associates at work and my last foster mom about it. I also called my aunt, and she told me my mom had a drinking problem and was not a very good person and that it wasn't the best idea. I contemplated for those few days.

I cried because I couldn't believe that she would cut me off that easily just because I wanted to think about it. I didn't want to lose my mom again, so I said yes when she finally called again.

CHAPTER 21

Two weeks after finding a woman I hadn't seen in seventeen years, she was moving in with me. She took the greyhound from Detroit to Grand Rapids, Michigan. I had no idea what she looked like. I arrived at the Greyhound and went inside with my boys. I saw a woman with a weave ponytail, a flowered shirt, and pale green capri pants on, looking at me.

She yelled out, asking me if I was Sophia. It was my mom. She looked nothing like me. I had wondered for years who I looked like, thinking it was my mom, and we looked nothing alike. I was very disappointed with the way she looked. I thought she would be a little bit older version of me. Drugs and alcohol had taken her looks away. She looked older than her age and wasn't dressed the hottest.

She stood about five feet six or five feet seven. She has very pretty silky hair. It was such an awkward meeting. She hugged me with no emotion. There were no tears shed from me or her. Seventeen years of not seeing your flesh and blood and you don't shed a tear? Weird. I looked at her face as I helped her gather the three bags she'd brought. She had three nose rings.

She had two in one nostril and one in the other. The earrings in her nose were big, studded earrings that you wear on the bottom of your ear. Her ears had about ten holes a piece. In every hole, there hung a huge loop earring, the kind you only put in the bottom hole.

She had sunglasses on. She never took them off to look me in my eyes. She exchanged no words of emotion or gratitude for me after locating her. I figured she kept her sunglasses on because her left eye is fake. My aunt had told me my mom had a nose ring after she'd seen mine on the pictures I'd posted on Facebook.

She also told me my mom's eye had been knocked out with a hammer. The man that my mom was heavily involved in drugs with hit her in the eye with a hammer, and she lost her eye. She later told me that it was a self-conscious thing for her. This lady was nothing at all of what I'd hoped and prayed for, but she was my mom, so I guess in a way she was who she was, my biological mother.

We exchanged hi's and hugs and went back outside to get into my truck. I took her to my apartment, and she went to sleep. She had arrived early in the morning so everyone was tired. My kids and I went back to bed as well. We all sat around and visited my mom for a while after we all woke up. She got up a little later and decided to walk around. She had been drinking and was feeling herself, so she wanted to interact with a male neighbor across the way.

She continued to drink like that all day every day. I was sick of it. I asked her repeatedly to stop being drunk in my home. I did not believe in drinking like that. When she got drunk, she was rude and would talk junk and yell at my kids the next morning because she would have a headache. I kicked her out, and she went to move in with my brother.

My brother had not even wanted me to look for my mom. He was bitter and angry about the life he had lived and said she was not worth looking for. So once she went to live with him, he started to treat her badly. He talked about her and her issues in front of all his friends and his girlfriend's family. My mom called me one day crying, and I let her back into my home.

She looked for a job but continued to get drunk. She found a job at McDonald's about a month after coming back. She spent her paychecks on booze and cigarettes. We were into it all the time. I felt like I was dealing with another child. She would try to cook and clean drunk and end up burning and wasting food and would half-clean everything.

There was not a day that went by that she was not drinking a big bottle of vodka. The entire bottle would be completely emptied within the hour she bought it. My mom found a friend at her job and would hang out at his house with his mother. The guy was a younger gay boy that she had befriended. She decided to move into the house with the boy's mother.

Thank God she was out of my hair but was still in the same city, so I didn't have to worry about her disappearing on me. She lived there for a few months until she and the woman got into it. No one wants to be around, let alone live, with an alcoholic; so the woman wanted her out. I let her come stay with me again.

By this time, I had moved into a three-bedroom home with hardwood floors. She had taken the third bedroom downstairs. I was going to help her find a roommate because her hours had been cut at Mc Donald's due to her going to work tipsy all the time. We found her a roommate on the other side of town from me.

I took her to the woman's house to visit and do an interview. The lady stated that she was a reformed alcoholic and said she didn't drink anymore. She had been sober for about fifteen years and didn't want to be around anyone that drunk. My mom told her that she didn't, and I didn't tell because I wanted her out my house.

The lady accepted my mom into her home. It lasted less than a month. My mom lost her job, and of course, the lady discovered her drinking issue. In the meantime, she had made up with the previous lady she had stayed with, so she moved back in with her.

A couple of months later, my son's father was shot in his stomach. They had come to the stepdad's house looking for my son's father. They gave the message to his dad by attempting to take his life away. This caused my son's dad great alarm and fear.

He rushed to the hospital and called me to come get our son from him there. Me being the sweet, forgiving person I was, I hugged him and told him to be careful and good luck. He just sat there crying and told me thank you and to hurry and leave; he didn't want me seeing him like that.

We got along for those last few weeks up until the day President Barack Obama was announced to have won the election. That day I remember all too well. It was seventy degrees outside, middle of November, and hot.

I had hardwood floors in my home, and it had just hit early afternoon. He stopped by to see his son. He came into my home and sat down on the couch next to my mom. He spoke to my eldest son who was on the potty and made conversation with me and my mom about the presidential election.

He played with our son for about twenty minutes then began to yell and curse at me. He stated that the house was too f—ing cold, and I was stupid and f—ing retarded, and he hated me. He told me to never call him again, that he was changing his number, and that I was to call his mom to have contact with him.

I sat in my kitchen and cried. He was treating me so bad, and I hadn't done anything to him. He just blatantly disrespected me in front of my mother and my kids. It was so instant, almost like he was bipolar, which I now believe he was. He stormed out my house and didn't speak to me for a week.

A week later, he called me from a new number. He stated it was his new number; I told him okay and hung up. He had just cursed me out and told me to never call him, so what was he calling me for? I had decided to take the Greyhound to Alabama to see my aunts and my sister for the first time.

My son's dad asked if he could keep our son for two weeks before I left because I would be gone with him for two weeks. I told him he could. Plus, my son's birthday was a day away, and he was having a separate party from mines. That same day, later on that evening, while I was at work, he was murdered.

No one called and told me anything. I did not find out until I went to pick my son up. Everyone was outside crying, and his mom was running around yelling in the yard. I thought there had been a fight. When I knocked on the door, my son's dad nephew answered, he told me that "they had gotten him." That "he was gone." He was referring to my baby's father; he had been shot several times in his car during a drug exchange.

CHAPTER 22

The day before my son turned one year old, his dad was taken away from him. My heart broke in half. I had never experienced such pain and shock in my life. I had been living from home to home my whole life; I had never experienced loss of anyone.

If anyone did die in my foster families, it wouldn't mean anything to me because they weren't family. I had this man's son—that meant a lot. I ran up the stairs of their town home into the bathroom and cried my eyes out. I didn't know what I was feeling; I had a variety of feelings and emotions hitting me at one time.

I grabbed my son and held him, crying and kissing him. I took him home and called all the ladies I worked with at the time. Everyone rushed over, hugging me and comforting me. They sat with me all night to the wee hours of the morning. I couldn't sleep or think. I sat up all night in shock, shaking my head and crying on and off until the next morning.

The next day was supposed to be a day of celebration for my son's first birthday, but it ended up being a day of mourning. His father's family called and wished him happy birthday; they stopped by and dropped a cake off his aunt had bought. They went back home because they were not emotionally stable to stay.

His funeral had quite a few attendees. His drug buddies and the females he had relations with were all there. I say drug buddies because none of them have called or done anything for his son since his murder. In the hood, the guys you deal with every day and come around your son all the time are supposed to look out for your offspring after your death. It's like a silent oath or pact between drug partners. No one has in the two and a half years he's been dead.

Anyways, I became a complete single mom. My son called me daddy for a full year after his father's death. I know he wondered what happened to his dad. Though he was mean to me all the time, he was a very good dad. He had his son all the time up until his death.

So it hurt me to know that someone would take his dad from him like that, especially on the day before his first birthday. My son's father also only had a week left before he was to be off parole. Funny how things happen, huh? They say everything happens for a reason.

I've been wondering for years, why? Why would he live that lifestyle? Why did he treat me so bad? Why would he cheat on me as I carried his child? All my whys will never be answered, so I pray.

I wonder why God would cause me to feel such guilt about getting the abortion, just for me to go through hell the entire pregnancy and then lose his dad. I just don't understand. I guess it's not for me to understand. I hope it all falls into place soon, and I will see the reason.

I've been in only one real relationship since my son's father's murder. I met this guy three days after his death. We weren't together at the time of his death, so I figured why put my life on hold. This guy was twenty-six years old, with six kids from four women, and he lived in a halfway house. Why I gave him my number, I have no idea. I tell myself that it was due to the fact that I was vulnerable because of the recent situation that had taken place.

He seemed like a nice guy. He talked good, and I decided to take a chance with him. He proved okay at the beginning. We spent a lot of time together. Every time he was allowed out the halfway house, he came to my home to spend time with me. My son grew very attached to him; this was the only man he was around right after his father died.

My new boyfriend got locked up a few months after we dated. I went to visit him every weekend and put fifty dollars in his commissary every week along with fifty dollars on my phone every week. I was trying to ensure that I was 100 percent supportive since my deceased baby's daddy had always told me I was a bad girlfriend.

Doing everything for this man did absolutely nothing for me. He began flirting and cheating via Internet social sites. I discovered this one day while going through his e-mails. I had seen the name of this site popping up on his e-mail for weeks but never thought anything of it. I finally decided to click on it.

My boyfriend was flirting and leaving nasty messages on every picture of his female friends. I had gotten a phone in my name for him a few months before, and he was using the phone I paid for to cheat and talk to other women. A woman called his phone one night. I was getting ready to take him back to the halfway house; the girl got nervous, stuttering over her words, and asked for a random female's name.

We got into it really bad that night. It almost became a physical altercation; after arguing and yelling for about twenty minutes, I let it go and told him to give me the key he had to my house. He refused, and when I grabbed his arm to snatch it, he pushed me into the door.

I gave up and took him home. I had his phone cut off. He called me from a friend's phone the entire night. He apologized repeatedly, asking me not to leave him, stating he was sorry and that he loved me. We made up, and I forgave him.

He got locked up again a few months later. I went to visit him, and one of his exes who had been harassing me for a month was there. This b— was beyond psycho. She would talk crap on my MySpace page. She hacked into my e-mail account and made up a fake account on Facebook and sent a friend request, just to pick.

I could not believe she was at the jail. While he had been telling her I was crazy, he had also been telling me she was crazy (which she was; I experienced it). He told me he had forgotten to take her name off his visitation list from his previous lockup before I met him. I forgave him again.

Things weren't the same from that point on. I could no longer look at him in the same way. I didn't trust him. He was sneaky and manipulative. He had breached my trust and my feelings, and I had lost intimate feelings toward him. He was locked up one more time during our odd relationship; this time I let go. I decided this was a sign for me to let him go and move on. That's what I did, but he wouldn't stop writing me, so I was kind of torn.

I met another guy in the meantime. He was in his mid-thirties, had a car, a job, his own place, and a drug hustle. He was doing well for himself, and he dressed well. I began to hang out with him. He stayed down the street from my godmom. On my twenty-second birthday, not one so-called friend called to say happy birthday or to hang out with me.

I had just met this man two weeks ago, and he spent my entire birthday night with me. He bought me scratch-off lotto tickets, about fifty dollars' worth, and a drink. I slept with him that night. Yes, I had learned my lesson from my last pregnancy and used protection; I had the depo shot as well.

We began to date and spend a lot of time together. He was a real gentleman. He took me out on dates all the time. He paid someone to move my furniture into a new house. He was a very good guy, but he was very controlling.

Due to the fact it was a twelve-year age gap, He treated me like I was a child. Every time I said something, I was being rude according to him. When I responded to something, I was talking back. It began to get annoying, but I dealt with it because his good out-weighed the bad. A few months later, I was pregnant.

Now, as I mentioned, I was on the shot. When I was with my high school sweetheart, I had gotten one shot and did not get pregnant for a full year. I assumed it would be the same this time around. I was wrong. I immediately decided to get an abortion. I knew I was ready to end "our thing" we had going on.

I was not about to have another child with no father in the home. I had my abortion done a couple of weeks after finding out. The baby's dad paid half of the bill, and I called a number I was given that paid a portion of the fee as well. We were never the same with each other. The situation caused a wall to build between us, and we split ways.

CHAPTER 23

I continued to just be single until my ex got out of prison. He came home, and I told him everything that happened. We talked it out and decided to move past everything he'd done and everything I'd done. Things were still tense between us regardless; we'd both lost each other's trust.

It lasted for about two months and for two weeks in a row. He would not come home for two and three days. I put his belongings on my front porch the last weekend he pulled that mess. He came and got his things and moved in with his aunt.

We talked constantly during our separation. It was decided that we just needed space from each other. He said he needed time to get himself together and get a job and stability going. It was official; we would still be together but will live separately. A few months later, I told him I missed him and wanted him back home. The next day, on Valentines, on Facebook, he was in a picture with another woman.

My man was in a picture between another woman's legs in a pool. He was holding her in a hot tub in another picture. So the day after I tell him I love him and wanted him back home (after all the pleading he had done, telling me he wanted to come back), he went and messed with another woman. What the hell?

When I saw those pictures, words cannot express how broken my heart and feelings were. He had the nerve to tell me she was a family friend. He stuck to that story for a month, then finally admitted he attempted to sleep with her that night they took the pictures, but he had his kids with him and couldn't proceed.

I finally let it go all the way. He wasn't worth the headache or drama. I could do better by myself. He didn't have a pot to piss in or a window to throw it out of. I decided to live the single life. I was always in and out of relationships. I had never just taken the time to relax and be alone.

It was time to get to know myself and realize my worth. I have been single for two and a half years now. Yes, I've been with a few different men on a sexual basis only. Committing myself to someone has been something I've yearned for, but I have fought the temptation.

CHAPTER 24

I allowed my mom to come stay with me again. She'd gotten into it with the lady she was residing with. When I picked my mom up, she looked horrible. She had lost so much weight. She claims it was from stress, but when she lived with my brother, he'd told me she still smoked.

With how small she had gotten within such a short amount of time, I was starting to believe him. Now even though I allowed my mom back into my home for the umpteenth time, her respect for me and my household was still no concern for her.

The most significant event with my mother occurred one day after asking her to watch my sons. I had an interview for a second job the following morning. I needed my mom to babysit for me so I could go. People asked me why I was allowing my mom to watch my kids when she'd lost seven of her own.

I assumed she would be a better person and not be drunk with my children. I have to admit though sometimes I would come home and find her drunk, on the few occasions I did ask her to look after them. Well, basically, the day before the interview, my mom had headed out to hang.

I called her at around 11:00 a.m. to remind her to make sure she was on the bus at a decent hour so she could get back to the house. She was drunk! Yes at eleven o'clock in the morning. I was pretty upset with her, and I shared my feelings about her early-morning binge.

She thought nothing of it, stating that she was a grownup and that she wasn't at my house, so whatever. The day went on, and it was almost eleven at night. I called her again to see where she was. She stated she was on her way; she was still drunk. By almost midnight, I figured that she was lying, and she had forgotten to catch the bus.

I was right. She had missed the bus and wanted me to wake my babies up and go get her. I told her no. I was not going to pick her up, and I did not want her watching my boys with a hangover in the morning. I stated that she would not be yelling and screaming at them all morning because of her decision to drink the entire day before.

I hung up on her and made some calls to locate a sitter for both boys. My eldest son's dad was fine with keeping his son. I called my youngest son's granny who had talked to my mom already.

I didn't understand why my mom befriended a woman who called her "crackhead" and threatened her daughter and called her daughter out her name?

That's crazy! A mother is supposed to be protective and defensive over their children.

My mom never once checked the woman over those evil words she'd spewed at me just the previous year before I found her. That bothered me from the beginning. Well my son's granny tried to convince me to go grab her. I told her no as well. I suggested she go get her if she was so worried.

She stated that she was going to. After talking for about a minute, her line beeped. She stated it was my mother and that I should hold on. She clicked back over, forgetting I was on the line. I could hear her tell her daughter that my mom said I called her out her name and dogged her and that she was going to go pick her up.

I silently hung up the phone. A half an hour later, my youngest son's granny was calling me again. She had went to get my mom and wanted to bring her to my home. I told her my mom was not staying at my house that night.

Every time my mom gets drunk, there's an argument or a fight about something. She brings up the pass and pisses me off. All the things I went through during our separation, I told her about. When she's drunk, she talks about how I'm not the only one who went through something.

Not about how sorry she is, I went through it because of her actions. She throws a one-man show, a pity party. Then she sits around and yells, talks to herself about all the kids she's lost, how her step dad beat her, and cries. I was not about to deal with that the night before an interview.

My son's granny took her home for the night. The next day, I dropped my youngest son off to his dad's mom. She tried to talk me into giving my mom another chance. She told me that even though my mom had never been there, she was still my mom. I told her, "You live the life I lived and then you tell me to keep putting up with some mess I don't have to put up with."

Nobody can tell me what to do when it came to my mom. For goodness sake, I took the woman in two weeks after finding her, and she showed no gratefulness or respect for my unconditional love for her. I went to pick my son up after the interview. My son's granny looked irritated with me. We spoke briefly about my mom and my son's behavior for the day.

She sounded weird and annoyed like I'd done something to her. Before I knew it, I was getting a phone call from my mom. She was flipping out, calling me "b—" and threatening to fight me. She stated that my youngest son's granny had told her everything—all the things I'd heard about my mom before finding her.

She also told her some recent information I'd told her about my mom. I had mainly complained about my mom's drinking problem. There was something else that, I can admit, I should not have told my son's granny. I thought daughters are supposed to tell their mom everything, though. I thought moms were supposed to keep all their daughter's secrets.

That's what I had seen on TV. Maybe I was wrong. I didn't know because I'd never had any one of my foster moms treat me like an actual daughter. She was pissed. Basically what happened was after my mom got there, she had told my son's granny everything I'd ever told her about her and her family.

Being that she was my mom and our relationship was still somewhat new, I figured a good mom would have just talked to me about it. My mom did the complete opposite and turned on me. Instead of approaching me and asking me about the situation, she wanted to physically hurt me. That was our first *serious* problem, and she didn't even go about it like a real mother. She went about it like a stranger or an enemy off the streets.

My youngest son's dad had shared some pretty gruesome stories about his family and his upbringing. By wanting that mother-daughter connection, I had shared everything with my mom to get her caught up on my life and the life of my son's father. She was my mom, and that's what daughters do—have deep and intense conversations with their mothers.

At least that's what I had been told from people with moms. Out of my mom's anger for not letting her into the house, she revealed every family secret she knew about them and my own genuine feelings toward family of my baby's father. Some things she blatantly lied about!

In retaliation to what she had heard, my youngest son's granny responded by telling my mom everything I had said about her. Basically, this sixty-something-year-old woman and my forty-five-year-old mother spent the night telling each other what I had said about the other one. How childish. I called my son's granny and asked her why she went and told my mom all that old stuff.

My son's granny instantly jumped in defense stating that I was running my mouth and she didn't give a f—. She told me, "F— you." She called me the b-word, ho, etc. I told her I wanted her to remove some things she stored in my basement. She cursed at me again, then she hung up.

I could not believe all the mess that was going on. It was like a bad dream. My mom teamed up with my enemy—against me? My mom started calling me that night. She called me the b-word, whore—anything she could think of. She threatened to fight me, and she and my son's granny were laughing about it.

The next day, she left a voice mail calling me names and said that she was going to fight me and that I better hide my truck because she was going to knock my windows out and slash my tires. Then she said the most dreadful words a mother can say to their child: "You were my demon child when I had you, you will always be my demon child." The exact words that were in the report!

That night, I muscled the strength to gather all her heavy bags and set them outside my back door. I originally threw her things all over the place but rethought my actions and picked the stuff up and placed her items to the side. I went up my basement steps about six or seven times to get her and my son's granny's things.

I called them the next morning as I was leaving for work and told them that their things were outside. My mom and my son's granny began cursing me out. I hung up on them and went to my first day of orientation. I'd gotten the job.

When I arrived home, their belongings were gone. I had just purchased a couch set a few weeks back and the plastic and cardboard were next to my back steps. On the cardboard, it read "F— you, b—!" One of these old women had really been immature enough to write profanity on my property! I grabbed the mess up and threw it into the trash. I listened to the missed messages on my home phone. My mom had left about four or five messages to threaten me.

She had previously sprained her ankle while walking around intoxicated that winter. She was going on about how I better watch my back. She was going to get me when I least expected it. She told me I was wrong for putting her out on a broken ankle. Now why in the heck would I let a woman who'd been threatening me for an entire day and night come back into my home? A home that she lived scotch-free in. A home that she had no respect for. A home that she caused constant problems and gave constant attitude in. A home that she was blessed to be allowed to stay in! She didn't deserve to stay in my home.

I was at my breaking point with her. After all those threatening messages, I'd had enough. I called and cursed her out to the fullest. Here she was, a homeless woman that I didn't even know and allowed to stay in my home, and this was the thanks I got? I let her know I was not afraid of her. With the life I've lived, there's not too much that can or should scare me.

I told her that if she really wanted to fight me, she could bring it. I was not going to allow a woman that I still didn't even consider my mother to keep threatening and disrespecting me. Her ranting and raving with no real retaliation from me was over.

I also brought up the fact that the lady she'd previously been living with had dogged her. My mom was complaining the lady owed her $50. She had told me that when she asked for her money back, the lady called her out her name and hung up on her. She never called that woman back.

I called her a coward for picking on someone that was less than half her age when she couldn't stand up to a woman her own age and size. That killed all her crap talking. I had gotten her where it hurt. She was picking on her own child versus a stranger in the street, and she was "soft" for it. I also called my uncle who told her he would drive from Detroit and beat her down if she laid a hand on me.

CHAPTER 25

My youngest son's granny has never shown me respect. After her son's death, I gave her money for the funeral. A month later, it was her birthday. I came to her party and bought her a bottle of Hennessy. Yes, this is after she came to my apartment and made the scene with her son.

I have given this woman food. One thing I do receive from the state is food stamps. I took this woman to the store before and bought her food because she had none. She told me she would give me cash back for the favor. She never did, and I never bugged her about it.

On top of that, I drove her to the store a few times because she had no gas. About three weeks later, she needed food again. Now I don't think I'm better than anyone, but I never have had the need to go to a food pantry. My youngest son's granny had already gotten her food for that month. I went and signed up for her and gave her all the food.

She was constantly having issues with money. Every time she needed to borrow money, I let her. If she needed a ride, I provided one for her. I was always to her rescue whenever she called me. My youngest son's granny lives in Tennessee.

Several months after the altercation with her, me, and my mom, she came back from Tennessee to visit. She and her daughter got into an altercation a couple of days after her arrival. She called me, bawling her eyes out. She repeated how hurt she was about the fight and the things her daughter had said to her.

Even though she'd never apologized for her previous behavior, I soothed her. I talked and encouraged her while listening to her pour out her heart and feelings. I told her she could stay her last three weeks at my home. She arrived about twenty minutes later, completely disoriented. I hugged her and brushed her tears away, letting her know it was okay, and I had her back. I told her I would pray for her, and I understood what she was going through.

To have one son be murdered two and a half years after he just gotten out of prison after doing six years and lose two more sons for murdering someone without the chance of parole on the same year you get the other back is hard to muster. I sympathized with a woman who constantly disrespected and mistreated me.

She came and stayed for two weeks in my home. I had no hard feelings toward her at all, and her stay was made comfortable. She cleaned and cooked when I went to work and watched the boys for me. It was nice having her there. She took off back down South, still never apologizing. She did, however, thank me for allowing her in my home in her time of need.

A couple of months later, I decided I was going to cut my son's hair. I told my son's aunt, who then called her mom. My son's dad had gotten another woman pregnant shortly after we'd broken up. I was leaving my son with my deceased baby dad's other baby mother. She had given birth to his son after his murder and would watch my son from time to time.

The other baby's mother called me upset that day. She told me that my son's family had called about the haircut. They did not want his haircut and was telling her not to take *my*—keyword —*my* son to the barbershop for me. She said she did not want to be in the middle of our feud, and she didn't know what to do.

I thanked her and told her never mind, that I'd take him when I got the chance. Not even fifteen minutes later, my son's granny called. She left a voice mail telling me she couldn't stand me, that I was a stupid b—, and that she wished her son would have never gotten me pregnant. She told me she wanted to fight me when she came back to town. She ended the voice mail, saying "b—" long and drawn out then hung up.

Wow, after all I had done for this woman; she could not find the decency or maturity to respect me. I still got *my* baby's haircut. This woman did nothing for my son but babysit him. She didn't buy him things for Christmas or his birthdays or anything (besides food)—period.

Who was she to tell me what to do? She wasn't the one who had to keep his hair braided, I did. It was something I did not have time to do. I was working two jobs, that's why I wanted it cut. I forgave her after that incident as well.

She came back to town again. She didn't fight me or attempt to. I let her visit and keep my son overnight for weeks at a time because I knew she missed him with living out of town and all. The people I associate with and knew about the drama she kept causing me and told me to keep my son away from her.

They said I am too nice to her, and that's why she keeps picking on me. I honestly think that if I had a mom with a backbone and some family, they would not keep picking on me. Out of all the women who had kids by her three different sons, I'm the only one who got hit with threats all the time. They know I have no big sis, cousin, mom, or aunt to tell them to back the hell off and mess with someone their own age.

I hit my breaking point with my son's granny on the spring of 2011. I am done with her and her unnecessary drama and bull. There's only so much a person can take, and I've taken all I can from her. This past spring vacation, she stated that she wanted to keep my son for the whole week that school was out.

That was fine with me. A week before she had gotten into it with her daughter again, she needed to borrow $20 for a rental application. I loaned her the $20 (which I never got back), and I drove on the other side of town, picked her up, and took her to the totally opposite side of town to drop her off at an in-law's house.

The weeks she was supposed to keep my son, she stated that I needed to pack him a bag full of food—a food bag with milk, juice, cereal, and whole meals. My son was only three at the time. How much could he possibly eat? I also wondered why would you attempt to keep your grandson and not have food for him?

I took him to the house of my eldest son's granny, and she's never asked for a dime, let alone food. She feeds him off her own food. Yeah, okay, whatever, I'll send him some food, no biggy.

She tells me her daughter is going to pick him up because she'd gone out of town. Her daughter came the next day to get him. I had just gone shopping the day before. Her daughter stated to wait until her mom came back. She would tell me what foods she wanted me to bring for him because they weren't going to be staying at her apartment when she got back.

I told my son good-bye and headed back into the house. His granny called later stating that she was staying with her daughter-in-law. She called from her daughter's phone because hers was cut off. She told me she didn't know the address or the phone number to where she'd be staying, and she would call me later so I could drop the food off.

She didn't call until the day after. When she called, I was at one of my jobs already. I figured the number that kept calling me had to be her. I didn't know the number on my caller ID, so I snuck into the restroom to listen to the voicemail. It was her. She left a message stating that she asked me to pack him a bag of food, that he was hungry, and that there was no food for him where she was at.

She said that the daughter-in-law was nice enough to buy him something to eat the day before, but now I needed to come through. She said she told me what to buy, and I should have had it together for him. She had the nastiest tone of voice on the message.

First off, she had told me she would call me so I could bring the food. Second off, her daughter told me to wait until her mom decided what foods she wanted for him. Third off, I'm not a child, I don't need anyone telling me "I told you" to do something. I'm *not* ten years old.

Last but not least, she always has to give me so much attitude. No matter how polite or cordial I am toward her, it's never enough for to be decent toward me. There's always a problem with her. She always makes things bigger than what they are. I thought you were supposed to mature with age.

I called her and told her I was at work, and she would have to wait because I was working both jobs that day. I also let her know I was tired of her constant attitude and disrespectful words toward me. Now I came at her so politely, so calmly, and so respectfully.

I expressed my feelings and took up for myself. She wasn't used to that. It made her angry. It's only so much one person can take before they've had enough and get fed up. She began to flip out immediately; I told her I had to go because I was sneaking on the phone to call her back. I hung up.

My phone rang several times after we ended the conversation. It was her. She left another voice mail. I took a break and went to listen to it. She was bugging out. Once again, I was called names and cursed out. She told me I was a bad person because my son's skin was f—ed up. He has eczema, so do I and my mother. (I guess his eczema is my fault.) He's always sick (he was in school with other kids; he's bound to get sick).

She said that every time she'd get him, he's always hungry (he was in school from morning to afternoon). He went to her daughter's house after school because I'd be at work, so how was it my fault he was hungry? Everything she said made no sense or was irrelevant. Of course, as always, she just wanted to stir up trouble.

She then said she was going to grandparent court. I never heard of it; think she made it up. She told me she was sick of all the baby mamas that her sons had, and she wasn't dealing with any of us anymore. She told me I could go down to court with her or she'd go by herself.

With all the voice mails I'd saved with her threats and ignorance, what judge would give her grandparent custody rights? She continued to rant and rave and dog me out saying I could have given her daughter some money to buy him some food. The previous week, I had let her borrow $20 for an apartment application fee. She owed me $20. So truth be told, if she was so concerned, she should have taken the money she owed me and bought him some food.

She continued her negative statements, asking me what type of mom drops their child off with no food to their granny—a lot of moms. Most grannies are typically able to feed their grandbabies. I told her I'd be picking my son up after work; I didn't want her watching him that week. She told me come get him right then and there.

I got off the phone and told my supervisors I had to leave due to a family emergency. They let me leave with no penalty; they could see I was extremely upset. I was just so sick of taking the crap from my son's granny! As I got in the car, I realized that there was another voice mail left by her. She called me out my name some more, and told me to be ready for a fight when I arrived at the home she was staying in.

I went and got my adoptive sister just in case something went down. This lady is like sixty-one years old. I would hope she wouldn't be trying to fight a twenty-three-year-old in front of my son. I assumed she had someone there to fight me for her since I didn't know who she was staying with or where she was.

I jumped on the highway, blood racing and heart beating fast. I called the last foster mom I'd lived with. She advised me to call the police. I had to be to my other job in two hours, and it wasn't worth losing my job over. I had just gotten that job and that was my first week out there for training. I worked too hard and took too many tests to be fired the first week for bad attendance.

My foster mom told me, after this incident, to stop dealing with them and stop allowing them to cause me so much stress and drama. They weren't worth it because they could do nothing for my son and the ruckus was being kept up too often. I told her I just didn't want to break him away from his family because I had none for him.

She told me I was going to have to get over it because she was tired of this family picking on me. I told her okay, hung up, and called the police. I called my son's grandmother to find out where she was. I didn't know the area, so I called the police back and they gave me directions to the home.

The dispatcher advised me to wait at the corner until I saw an officer pull up. I did. Once I saw him, he gave me the go-ahead to go down the block, and he trailed me. As I pulled up, her daughter was pulling up behind the police. She jumped out of the car yelling and screaming.

Her daughter was furious, yelling at me about why I called the police. Her older son came out with my son and told his mom to not even talk to me and leave. She continued to ask why the police had been called. I told her if she was in my shoes and was invited to a strange place and didn't know who lived there, she would too.

She brought up the fact that this was not the first time her mom had threatened me. Exactly. My point exactly. She furthermore proved my point by stating her mother was in her sixties and she needed to mature and stop picking on others. I didn't deserve it, and I never did anything to the woman to get the disrespect she had constantly been lashing out on me—that she just wanted to talk crap to me like she always does and I didn't need the police for that. My sister jumped out the car thinking my son's aunt was too close to my face. My son's granny began to call her fat and the b-word. My sister flipped immediately.

She began to argue with the granny. Curse words flew back and forth while her daughter tried to interrupt, telling her mom to go back in the house. She would not listen. She continued to stand outside and yell and curse. My sister was relentless after her blatant disrespect toward her. My son's granny wouldn't let her have the last word either. So it just continued on until the cop started yelling.

Her daughter was upset that my sister would not be quiet, so they began to argue. I had to calm her down and tell her to get back in the car. My sister was getting angrier by the minute. It took a lot of me yelling over my sister for my sister to calm down. After about two or three minutes of persuasion by me and the cop, she got back in the car.

My son's aunt continued to try and reconcile the situation, but I'd had enough of her mom. I got in my car and left. My son's aunt called me once again asking why I had called the police on her mom. She stated that the house was not her mom's and her sister-in-law had never had any altercations with police at her house and she would be mad.

That was not my problem, I explained to her. Her mom cannot go around threatening and treating people any kind of way. She is way too old to keep drama stirred up all the time. She agreed with me and said she had been trying to talk with her mom about changing her ways.

I was talking to her on my cell at my foster mom's house. I had asked my foster mom if she would watch him for me. My foster mom was looking at me and shook her head the entire time. She mouthed for me to hang up the entire call. I got off the phone, and she explained her reasoning to me about disowning that family.

She told me that they were trying to drag me down so I could be on the level that their family was on, and they were getting closer to completing their mission. She told me that enough was enough, and I needed get a restraining order on them because I had proof of all the drama and threats. I told her I would.

After leaving her home, the aunt called again. She wanted to know where my son was so she could pick him up and take him to her apartment. I was very hesitant about the situation. I felt a trust with her just because of her maturity with trying to rectify the situation earlier.

I didn't quite know my foster mom's address. I just drive and go by landmark, not numbers. I gave her a made-up address that was close to the real one. She must have found the house because my foster mom begins to call my phone back to back an hour later.

I was at the other job by that time. So I headed into the hallway to take the call. She stated they were outside her home knocking. She told me the police were down the street and she was going to call them on her if I didn't want him going. She asked me if I'd given them her address. I told her no because I don't know it.

My son's aunt beeped in on my other line telling me she was outside. I let her know I was on the phone with my foster mom telling her it was okay. My foster mom reluctantly let him out the door to them. She told me to be careful and that I better stop letting them run over me.

I haven't talked to my son's granny since. She hadn't been back to town since the incident either. My son's aunt has only watched him about three times since the incident and that was back in April; it's now October. She told him she's going to get him, and she didn't show up.

She told us she's going to buy him some shoes but never did. She's going to take him to Chuck E. Cheese and never does. They have bought him three family dollar outfits—one coat and a hat and a pair of clothes. That's all I have ever seen them buy him.

When she needed to borrow money for gas, I let her; when her car broke down on her, I came to her rescue and jumped her car, but she keeps breaking her word to my son. Out of his three and a half years on this earth none of his granny, grandpa, or aunt has bought him any toys for Christmas or his birthday.

Yet they continue to call me a bad parent. Wow, the nerve of some people. It's amazing how much you can do for people, and they still show no gratitude or respect or thankfulness for having you in their lives.

CHAPTER 26

I wasn't going to include this part, but this is a biography, so I changed my mind. Late last year, December 18, 2010, to be exact, was the first time I had slept with a man the exact same day that I had met him. Our intended one night stand turned into a brief relationship.

This was different. It was a party for my god mom's birthday. We all went to the house of her boyfriend's aunt who had a little makeshift bar and club area in her basement. We danced and drunk the whole night.

He was a guy that caught my attention. He was the only decent-looking man in the room. A slow song had come on, and he gave a stripper performance to a girl at the party. He really had my attention then. I had not engaged in sexual activity for a while before that night. I sat in my chair all night and just watched. He made his way over to me after an hour or so. He sat down and introduced himself, saying his name was Kelon and that he was from Detroit.

We made conversation majority of the night until about one thirty in the morning. I really liked him and wanted to sleep with him but was unsure about it. I talked to my god mom about my feelings. She told me I was too young to always be so scared to try things. She told me to do whatever I felt.

She said I was a grownup, and there was nothing wrong with stepping outside the box every now and then. I took her advice and decided I would. We left that party and went to another. We were there for about an hour. He asked if we were going to hook up or not. He was getting impatient.

After about two hours of deliberation, I decided I would. I stopped at the store on my way home to grab some condoms. We headed to my house and sat on the couch. For another hour, I contemplated my decision again.

I grabbed the condoms and told him to follow me upstairs. We engaged in sexual activity. He was decent, so I wasn't too disappointed, but I felt nasty and used. I just knew he would never call me after this. No man wants to be with a woman that allows him to get with her on the first night.

I was wrong. Kelon claimed he liked me a great deal and would keep in touch. He went back home to Detroit the next day. I dropped him off at family house the morning after our encounter. I had a dream that night that he was going to play me. He called the next day. He told me that someone had broken into his apartment while he was gone and stole all of his things including his daughter's Christmas gifts.

I felt so bad for him. He told me that his phone was broke so he had it cut off, and he would be calling me from other people's phone until he got a new one. He told me that he was coming back to Grand Rapids after Christmas to stay with his aunt and her boyfriend in some woman's house.

The day before he came, he called me, telling me that his aunt had gotten into with the woman, and he couldn't live there anymore because she'd put his aunt out. I was very sad and devastated. I suggested that he stayed with me until his aunt found a new place for him to stay. He agreed.

That was my first mistake. He had no money due to his house supposedly being robbed; I went online and paid for his Greyhound fare—second mistake. He came with his one suitcase of clothes and shoes. I went to the store and bought him some hygienic things— third mistake.

On New Year's Eve, I suggested that we go out to eat and stay in and watch movies at home. Fourth mistake, I paid for our meal. We left and went to the house of my god mom's boyfriend's aunt to finish the night out.

There weren't many people there, but his aunt and her boyfriend were. They came over with some of his other family members and introduced themselves. His uncle started a conversation with me and kept touching my thigh right above my knee.

I thought nothing of it, thinking he was the type of person to use his hands while talking. My new live-in boyfriend thought otherwise and became pissed. He cursed him out saying that he was trying to hit on me.

Then he got mad at me and asked why I didn't tell him he was touching my knee. I guess my boyfriend's brother had seen the touching and told him. I stated my innocence, and he continued to fuss about it even though less than two hours ago he had told me he loved me.

He was in love in three weeks? Amazing! (Sarcasm.) We left the party with him fussing all the way outside. His uncle was outside with his aunt. He began to go off on his uncle over me. I kind of liked his jealousy; it made me feel good.

His aunt attempted to calm him. She told him to respect his elders. He would not listen. I tried yelling out for him to calm down. He told me to be quiet because I should have said something. Finally, his brother convinced him to get in my truck so we could leave. We headed home. I called my home girl, and my foster sister was staying the night, so we all got a board game out and some drinks and just had fun.

Then he got mad about something else. He went upstairs. I followed a few minutes later because he never came back down. He was lying down in the bed. He had taken his clothes off and everything. I asked what was wrong and once again tried to smooth the earlier situation.

Kelon was not budging from his standpoint, so I left. He came down the steps in a towel and sat with his legs wide open. Fifth mistake, I cursed him out for his rude and indecent behavior.

I was beginning to think either he's drunk or crazy. His eyes were bloodshot red, and he was acting nutty. Everybody decided it was time to put the game up. Game over. My girl left. My sister went to my furnished basement where she slept, and his brother slept on the couch. I headed upstairs to deal with his weirdness. We didn't talk about much, and I went to sleep.

The next morning, he apologized for his behavior. He told me that he had insecurities because of a previous relationship with his daughter's mother. He stated she cheated on him the whole time, and he didn't trust women. I accepted his apology and took his brother home. We continued to fuss and fight all the time after that first event.

This man stayed angry and upset about anything and everything. Every time I turned around, he was in a funk. I couldn't say or suggest anything to him without offending him. He wanted me to buy him Black and Mild's every day. I was trying to help him find a job. Once again, I found myself allowing another man to live off of me. This man raised his voice and got in my face so many times I just knew he was going to hit me.

I kid you not, almost every other day we were into it—bad. I kept forgiving him. I let him keep his daughter at my house for two weeks straight and everything. Several times he attempted to walk out on me, and I would get him back.

I don't know why I did. He wasn't doing anything but only use me and stress me out. I guess, after being single for two years, it felt good to have a man in my house. He was always cooking, cleaning, ironing, and doing laundry. He was very helpful around the house.

However, he had issues. I began to question rather or not he was bipolar. I had seen him flip out on his mom in front of me the second day after he'd come after Christmas. One night after dealing with his craziness, I decided to call his mom. His mom was a very polite woman who gave me the whole story of this man.

She told me the baby mama had used him and hurt him real bad, that he was actually homeless in Detroit living in some broken house a man let him rent for about $20 a month. She told me he had horrible anger issues and needed anger management classes. I also found out he had been in trouble with the law and was on probation.

The last week before his daughter left, he asked if his brother could stay the night. I told him yes. His brother stayed the next night and the next. The next thing I knew, it had been an entire week. He asked if I would drive his daughter and brother back to Detroit.

I told him no. He cursed me out for asking why his brother was still in my home. What? Seriously? I allow you to come to my home, bring your daughter to stay, and let your brother stay a week and you're still complaining. I could not believe my ears.

His mom had given me all the red flag, but I still kept him around. We got into it so many times, I honestly can't tell you, guys, what half of it was about. He attempted to leave again about a week or two after his daughter went back home. It was like negative five degrees out.

He had no money, no family here (his brother lived with someone too), no car, and was dragging a big ole suitcase plus his daughter's Dora luggage bag (that he'd forgotten to send back) with him. I convinced him to come back and stay because it was bad outside. We made up the next day.

Our "weird," way-too-quick relationship continued, and we didn't argue for a few days. Then one day after I discovered he only talked to his baby mama after I'd leave the house, I confronted him. That caused another big argument. I asked him so politely, not accusing of him of anything, just wondering why.

I was furious at Kelon for the constant complaining and disrespect in my house. These people I kept taking in my home kept trying to run my house. They kept trying to run me, and they all had disrespected me at some point and time and got away with it.

He complained the entire night. I got sick of it, so I told him he ought to be glad I let his daughter and brother stay. They were using my electricity and watching my cable while I went to work, all three of them. How dare he act out in front of his brother by yelling and cursing at me?

A few weeks later, he tried to get me to give him a $150 to go to Detroit to perform a rap with his friend. That was too much money to risk losing. He still hadn't paid me back his bus ticket money. I wasn't going to take that chance. I told him I would not give him the money for Detroit. That made Kelon the angriest I'd ever seen.

He complained and talked mess the entire evening. I got tired of hearing his voice and told him to call and ask his baby mama. He began to yell at me, telling me to keep her name out my mouth. This was the second time he had gotten angry with me for saying anything about her. He then called me a crazy b—. It was over! I had enough! I went crazy on him!

We both began to yell and curse at each other. I pointed out his entire dilemma. The fact he was homeless, a psycho, had no money, and had no job; and I had been there for him. He got in my face and began to make threats because I told him he had to go right then and there.

He said he would destroy my house if I put him out. I told him I was going to call the police. He acted like he was still going to do something. I called my ex on the phone to alert him of the situation.

I called my foster mom next. She had been the mediator in a lot of our crazy disputes. She told me to let him go, that enough was enough. She knew I was trying to make it work with him, and he obviously wasn't appreciating my dedication to help him get on his feet.

I told him he had to go, no ifs, ands, or buts about it. He got on my home phone and called his mother telling her about the situation. She cursed him out and told him to put me on the phone.

I told her about the disrespect he'd shown me twice just for saying his baby mama's name. I never disrespected the girl, called her out her name, or anything, but he'd attacked me both times just for referring to her. I told Kelon's mom I believed he was still in love with her because no man gets that mad over someone they don't care about. She agreed with me and told me to do what I had to do concerning her son.

She told me that she was tired of him calling and complaining to her. Kelon told his mom that I just made him sit in the house all day, and we never did anything. He had no money, no car, and didn't know anyone. I don't understand how he could blame those issues on me. I got off the phone with his mom and began to gather his stuff. He tried to keep me from gathering his stuff, saying he could do it himself.

Eventually, he began to cry and beg me not to put him out. He got on his knees and begged me. I ignored him. He continued to cry and beg for another chance, but I had enough. I stuck to my word. This man dropped to his knees again, asking where he was supposed to go with no money and no friends because it was late and there were no buses running. I told him I did not care. He pulled the player card out. He yelled about how much he loved me, and if he had a ring, he would marry me that week.

I laughed at him and told him to get up. I was enjoying the little act he was putting on. It was a funny scene. It was an insincere act, and I wasn't listening. He called his mom again who told him that if he wanted to make it right, he better suck my toes. I didn't know she had told him this until I felt his mouth on my toes. I got on the phone with her, and she began to laugh telling me she had given him that advice.

Like an idiot, I forgave him again. In my mind, I thought he was a good man because he cleaned and cooked, ran me bathwater, massaged my back, and did other pampering. What I should have been looking at was all the negative aspects. I was so desperate to have a man in my home I overlooked everything else. He had no car, no job, no money, and no respect for me. I let that slide just because no man had ever catered to me.

I dealt with his bull a little longer. We had a silent beef the night before Valentine's. That night, I decided I was done with him. That night, he presented me with chocolates, a stuffed animal, and a card. I accepted them thanked him. We did nothing romantic that night. I had lost my attraction to him because of all the stress he had caused me.

The next morning, I broke up with him. I bought him a bus ticket back to Detroit and dropped him off at the Greyhound station. I was still being nice and helped him. It's just my nature.

Two weeks later, I discovered I was pregnant. I knew the exact night I'd conceived. I could not believe it. The night I assumed it might happen, I had looked at an ovulation calendar and everything. The dates matched up to ovulation, and all that other stuff basically showed that I would not get pregnant for a few more weeks.

I decided to hurry and get my birth control shot the following week after the night we engaged in sexual activity, thinking I'd gotten it in time. The test was negative at the doctor's office that day because it was only a week and a half when I got the shot. So I had unintentionally gotten a shot while I was pregnant.

I had to move into my new place. I was pregnant and had just kicked my unborn child's father out. I said I would keep this baby. My boys were getting older, and I had already gotten an abortion two years before that.

I moved with help from only two people: my eldest son's dad who works third shift (he was already tired) and my god mom's oldest son. I tried my hardest to help, but I was so sick and tired. There were supposed to have been more people helping, but no one came through.

I spoke with someone at the planned pregnancy center. It was an older black female who told me her story of her having three kids out of wedlock before she met her husband. She told me my baby was a blessing and a gift from God and that I should keep it. I told her I would because I was a strong black young woman. I received my prenatal and stressed for about three weeks. I told everybody I knew and got their opinions about my situation.

I called my ex and told him the news. He wasn't excited because we'd just broken up and he had no financial security to support me or a baby. I was kind of hurt, but I knew he had nothing so I couldn't expect much. I told him I was keeping the baby. We talked every few days. He would just check up on me and let me know what was going on with him. He never asked me how I was feeling.

We talked about maybe getting back together so I wouldn't be a single mother of three. I told him he had to change a bunch of his ways for it to work. He told me I had issues too and I had to work on mine. We discussed the issues that caused our breakup. He told me he was not coming back until he had gotten a job down there or had made some money some type of way. He told me he was going to sell some drugs to make some quick money to survive until he found a job.

A few weeks later, he called me with a sad sob story, stating that he had lost some of the main drug man's product. He said that he was hiding from him because he had no money to give the lost product, price value, back.

He had lost the product that day because he had seen the police following him and took off running. He threw his products out while running, which put him in a hole. He was basically trying to get the money from me. I told him to be careful and watch his back. That was all I was offering.

The following week, he called to tell me he had the problem squared away. His baby's mother had given him the replacement money. I asked if he was sleeping with her. He told me no but stated that he ought to because she saved his life. I hung up on him. I texted him; I was okay. I was messing with someone else already anyway. Boy, did that get him going. He went psycho!

He called me about three times. On my voice mail, he called me whore, slut, b—, nasty, and a slur of other degrading names. He told me that no man wanted me anyway with two kids by two different men. He said I was going to be spending my life searching for somebody to love me with two children.

Who just wants a homeless, broke man? Isn't that the kettle calling the pot black? There were several statements about me aborting the pregnancy. He said he didn't care about the pregnancy; it probably wasn't his anyway, that I had to get rid of it because he wasn't going to be there.

I retaliated and cursed him back out through text. I put all of his flaws and issues in my text and told him he had some nerve. He then began to act like his baby's mother was texting me. He started threatening me, pretending it was her. He told me he was going to come back and knock my door in and beat me up. He continued name-calling and threatening me for about an hour until I told him I was going to have someone wait at my house to knock him out. That shut him up.

A couple of weeks later, I decided to get rid of the baby. I did not want to raise two kids with no father. I contemplated and cried for about two weeks. I didn't know what to do. I really wanted this baby, but I didn't feel I could handle two on my own. He was threatening me and treating me like crap. I was scared to do the pregnancy alone and raise a baby alone again. I set up my appointment. I cried that entire week.

I went to my appointment, and there weren't enough people there to get the doctor to come in. They took my info and my $425 and took my blood tests and ultrasound. I was told I had to wait until Monday. My appointment was on that Friday. I took it as a sign that God wanted me to keep that baby because I was having a hard time getting rid of the baby, and now my appointment was delayed.

I debated changing my mind and getting my money back. Then I made my mind up. I had to do it. I'm so alone with my son, and I didn't want to have another baby with no family there. The baby's dad lived in California, and the other family members were in Detroit. I couldn't bear struggling any further.

I got the abortion that Monday. I cried as I took my bottoms off. I cried as the doctor set up the equipment. I cried as he inserted the tube. My heart broke in half when I heard my fetus get sucked out into the tube. My breath was taken as tears escaped from my eyes. I wanted to take it back immediately.

It was over. The doctor looked at me on his way out and stated that he could tell I'd had a hard time making my decision. He told me it would be okay and walked out. I slowly got up and begin to cry again as I got dressed. I walked to the resting room and laid down, shivering and crying.

I was due on October 16, 2011. I just know it was my first my girl. My heart has been hurting ever since. I was ten weeks at the time, so I knew that the baby was only the size of a dot so that took a little of the guilt away. It's amazing to me that on that very day, I decided to get baptized for the first time, without realizing that I was due to have a child on that day. They say God works in mysterious ways. The day a child was to be born to me, I was born again.

To this day, I still cry about my baby I killed. I regret it from the bottom of my heart. I hurt all the time just thinking about my decision. It was not worth the hurt and void I feel now. If I could take it back, I would. A lady who invited me to the church where I was baptized said the significance of the baptism and expected due date was God's way of telling me that he forgave me for it and to let it go. I kind of think so too. I am human though, so it still does get to me from time to time. I just pray that when God sends me a husband, he would send that same baby back to me.

CHAPTER 27

Even though my youngest son's father is deceased, he still has a father figure in his life. Weston has stood up to the plate. He takes his son and my son when I go to work or if I just need a break. I am completely and utterly thankful for his caring and understanding of me and my son's situation. My son had a lot of behavioral issues due to always feeling left out and alone, same as I did when I was younger.

It breaks my heart every time my youngest son asks me to find him a daddy or asks where his daddy is. With Weston deciding to become involved in my youngest son's life full-time, I think it will calm him down a great deal. I hope that Weston is able to fill the void in my son's heart brought on by the loss of his father.

I feel horrible that I have no family for him to make him feel completely supported. His father's gone, his uncles are in prison for life, and his aunt has her own kid and her own life and she doesn't attempt to get to him too often. His granny, who would keep him all the time after his father's death, moved out of state.

I try to be a mother, a father, a cousin—anything—for him; but I'm only one person. I can only do so much by myself. So it's just me and my son against the world. United we stand, and I'll never let him fall, if I can help it.

I try to show him as much love as I possibly can. I don't want my son to fall prey to the street like his father. I strive to let him know one person can have all the love in the world for him. He doesn't need to seek out the love and the sense of belonging by joining any gangs or running the streets. People look at my son sometimes and say they see that he's a handful, that he looks bad.

No matter what my son's family background is, my son will never follow in his father's footprints. It's not in his genes no matter what anyone says. My son will grow up to be something in his lifetime. I refuse to allow anything less from him. There's a calling God has on his life. I refuse to believe that I went through nine months of hell with his father and lost his father, "just because." My baby was given to me for a reason. I know he's going to be a blessing to me and others he meets along the way.

I mentioned earlier that I had found my adoptive parents and had become involved in their lives again. My reason for the search was to spend time with my dad. About a year after this initial reconnection, I saw my adoptive mom's biological son at a bar. I was tipsy that night and spoke my mind. I asked him why didn't anyone report or say anything to his mom about the child abuse we were suffering at the time.

I guess a few months later, he must have thought about it and told his mom about our conversation. I stopped hearing from her soon after that encounter; I had no idea why. I saw one of my adoptive brothers, and he told me he had talked to our adoptive mom, and she said she wasn't dealing with any of us any more (I had reconnected him with her as well when he turned eighteen). She told him about what I'd said to her son.

I continued to call and leave messages up until a month or two before beginning to write this book. Three weeks before I decided to write my book, I received a message on Facebook. My cousin from when I was adopted told me my adoptive dad was slowly dying.

I had a lot of his family as my friend on Facebook. She was the only one that reached out to me and let me know what was going on. She told me she felt that I should know because she knew how much he meant to me and how much we meant to him.

I began to immediately inbox her all the questions that came to mind. Where is he? Why is he dying? How long has he been dying? She told me that she didn't know to much more than the fact he was dying. She had no idea where he was or why he was dying. I instantly began to cry and yell.

My heart was so sad and broken. I hadn't seen him in over a year, and now he was leaving me. I wrote my cousin telling her my thoughts; she offered me words of advice and encouragement. She said that if she found out anything else, she would let me know.

He passed away a couple of days after I'd heard. I had called and left messages on my adoptive mom's voice mail in the meantime. She still never called me or returned my messages even with this terrible situation. My cousin inboxed me the news. I can't explain the rush that came over me.

I cried out in pain. I continued to cry for the next two hours until my tear ducts were dried up. She told me she didn't know what they were planning as far as the funeral arrangements were concerned, and she'd keep me updated. She inboxed me her phone number so I could stay connected.

Around three days later, while at work browsing Facebook, I saw my dad's family members discussing that his "home going" was taking place. I was instantly upset and wondered why my cousin hadn't let me know when it was. I texted her immediately; she told me that she had no idea the funeral was that day.

My adoptive mom had planned everything so quickly and secretly that a lot of the family members had no idea. So I didn't get to say bye or see him before he passed. I was so hurt. No matter our differences or problems, I should have been able to see my dad before his passing or at least before he was laid to rest.

So I'm going to say my good-bye now. I love you, Dad. You meant the world to me. You made me feel like I belonged to you, like I was your flesh and blood, not a stepchild. You always made me laugh and smile with your silliness and stuttering when you were trying to joke around.

You were the only father I've ever had, and for that, I love you. You will always hold a special place in my heart and soul. You had genuine love for me, and my love for you was and will forever be genuine. God bless you; I know you're up there with him. My love will continue on for you. You will never be forgotten, Dad. I love you!

CHAPTER 28

I get extremely lonely sometimes. A lot of times I suffer from deep depression. It seems that from the time I was born, up until twenty-four years later, I was destined for doom. My life seems to be nothing but a never-ending sad story.

I can honestly say that I don't remember having a good year during any period of my life. I've never had a year of pure happiness and enjoyment of my life. Everyday life is a struggle for me. My past plays a big part on that. I've found my family but only communicate with my mom and one of my uncles. All that searching and wondering, and every day I still feel alone. I feel as if I never found my family.

I struggle with anxiety as well. I suffered from anxiety attacks quite often, but I've overcome that problem. I've learned to calm down and just breathe. Sometimes I just wonder why I was put on this earth so alone and deserted. Why is every day a stressful day for me?

I would love to wake up and just smile and be happy. It never happened; I hope one day it will. I'm looking and waiting for happiness. I want to feel normal. I always wanted to go over my "cousin's house," to call my nieces and nephews and to stay the night at my mom's house. I lack a lot of love and the sense of belongingness because of the life I've lived.

My mom suffers from a severe drinking problem. I promised her I would try to help her the best way I can once I get the funds. Even though she never contributed to my upbringing, I want to contribute to her well-being. I love her and honor her for giving birth to seven kids.

There are some people in this world who have my biological brothers and sisters and feel blessed to have them. I try not to control my mom, but her mind-set is not where it should be for a woman her age. Her alcohol has been taking control of her life for years, and she knows no other way but to be impaired.

I try to guide her and include her in my daily activities to divert her attention from the bottle. As "her child," I can only do so much. I do not encourage nor enable her addiction. I do not believe in wasting a life. Life is hard, but it's considered a blessing to many, and we are to embrace it and try to make the best of it.

I feel bad when I yell and basically chastise her about her unhealthy behaviors. As her daughter, I feel as if I have to be an example for her, versus the other way around, but I love her. I tell her every time I lecture her about her habit, that if I didn't love her, I wouldn't care. I care. I will always care.

It's kind of odd having a mother in your life that's never been a part of your upbringing. I feel as if I've found an old friend. My mom is a flighty woman who stays in and out of shelters, drinks, smokes marijuana, and does whatever she feels. She's not concerned about anyone but herself. Her selfishness causes me to feel as if I'm not her daughter but a person just passing through her life.

There is no constructive real-life conversations or advices she gives. When she does offer anything as far as words of wisdom or encouragement, she turns the conversation on her. It's always about what she went through as a kid. I never felt like my mom just said a genuine *sorry*, she didn't try to protect me.

I believe that's her way of making it seem as if her decisions were right. She struggles with extreme depression and low self-esteem, and her outlet for relaxation is being drunk all day, every day. I try to encourage her to do other things with her time. I complain and bug her every time she's impaired, hoping one day she'll get sick of me in her ear and just quit.

It never happened. A voice of reason can only do so much. The person with the problem has to be willing and should want to change their ways. I'll keep bugging and bothering her until I'm able to get her the type of help she needs.

I have a hard time showing affection to my children because of the fact that I've never experienced it. Most children sleep in the bed with their moms and play with her hair while watching TV; I never did. Most kids know majority or all their siblings; I don't.

There are a lot of things that are missing from my heart. I have voids that can never be filled because it's too late. I would like to fill this void with an open, loving group home for able-bodied women that just need a little boost.

My dream and ambition is to become successful as I possibly can. During the seven and a half years that I've been on my own, I have housed and supported seven individuals. All these people were grown and fully able adults. They all just needed a little help. They needed someone to house them in their time of need. I did. I love helping others out that are trying to help themselves. I always wanted and wished for someone just like me to be there for me.

It never happened. The ones that should have been there to support me didn't care. The few that shouldn't have had to do anything for me were the ones that would try and do the most they could for me. I want to be the boost.

I hate to see anyone in need or hurting. If I can help those hurting, struggling young women that are trying to get ahead in life, I will. I pray that with God by my side, I get to that point in life where I can make a difference in other women's lives.

The first time I ever asked for public help with rent, I was told I had to get an eviction. You mean to tell me I have to be near the pits of homelessness to get help? Why? I didn't want the help that bad. I will and would never subject myself to such matters for a little bit of money. It's not worth it. I'm a hardworking woman that just needed a little boost, and I had have nothing to get it.

While there are many young African American women just living off welfare and state programs and doing nothing to get ahead in life, someone who is working for a living is denied any type of help. That's not right or fair. So if I ever get the finances to start my homes, I'm definitely going to do it.

A lot of hardworking women deserve that help and opportunity. What's better than being allowed to live rent-free until you have the money to take care of yourself and children? I want to be the one who does allow them that opportunity.

I continue on with my life. I'm a twenty-four-year-old mom with two children, five and four years old. I rent my own five-bedroom home and own my own car, a Mazda 6. I've been working two jobs for the past two years, and I go to school whenever I get a break to go back. I am determined to finish getting my business administration degree.

I have about a year left in my community college. My goal is to finish within the next two years with God's help. It's pretty hard having a child with whom I get no help with. I have to survive, and to do that, I have to work hard.

I'm focused on keeping a roof over my boys' head and clothes on their back. No one or anything can disrupt my focus. My number 1 goal is to protect and provide for me and my family. No one is important to me at this point and time of my life. I've cut quite a few people off in my life.

I have learned that I worry too much about others—what they think of me, what they say about me, things that I shouldn't care about. I've been in so much drama trying to appeal to others or fit in I should say. Stopping my interaction with a lot of people has given me a new self-confidence.

I no longer worry about what other people think or say. There was one point and time when I wouldn't walk to the store without going with someone because I didn't want people to look at me. I wouldn't go into a grocery store by myself unless I had my kids for company. I've had over six different people live with me that I supported, men and women, because I didn't want to be alone. I struggled with being happy by myself for years. I'm so over it.

The entire summer that I've been writing this book, I've went everywhere with my kids and by myself. I figure, so what if someone talks about me? I'm beautiful; it's bound to happen. So what if a girl decides she wants to roll her eyes at me for no reason? Even if I walked with someone, she's still going to roll her eyes, regardless.

I can't go through my life trying to find and make someone my friend just so I won't feel alone. At the end of the day, I still felt alone even when the few people I used to call my friends were around. I'd rather stress about being alone because I am alone. For me, to stress over why someone isn't there for me is unnecessary stress, and I've taught myself to let it go.

I refuse to center my life around others. The only people I have to live for is myself and my children.

Everyone else and all the fake females I've dealt with along the way and have kept me in drama can kiss my black butt. They are no longer part of my life and I've moved on and grew up.

Yes, I have had an ultimately horrible life. Yes, I have been through hell and back. Yes, I am probably going to go through more. I have been through what some people could never handle. I am a strong individual that has kept moving through life each day trying to get ahead. I just want to be as successful as God will allow.

To all those that have walked a mile in my shoes or that has been through worse, keep your head up. Nothing is worth giving up on your life. Self-respect, dignity, and willpower are necessities to make it through this cruel word. Yes, it is very hard to not give up. Giving up is easier than trying, but giving up gets you nowhere while trying gets you one step closer to your goals in life.

Remember, life is not easy. Life will never be easy. Life is according to what you do to better it. Once you give up on life, you give up on happiness and a better life. Trust me, I know. I've been there, done that, and I'm still standing. My journey will continue as long as I'm on this earth.

All I can do is pray that God walks with me through it. You have to trust, have faith, and put your mind to what you want your life to be and become. It's all about mind power and willpower. Stay encouraged, my readers.

All smiles and love over this way. With the grace of God and the new me that I've discovered, I'm invincible. I'm a great and fun-loving person, and that right man and real friend will find their way to me. I don't have to look for it. I'm good. I'm grown, independent, smart, beautiful, and talented. I'm good!